CAMBRIDGE FIRST CERTIFICATE

PRACTICE TESTS

for the First Certificate in English Examination

Nicholas Stephens

Contents

What makes this Practice Test Book different from other test books available?

This book is different because it is more than just a book of practice tests. It has been designed not only to give students ample and realistic practice of the format and content of each part of the Cambridge First Certificate in English Examination (FCE), but also to provide useful vocabulary expansion and relevant advice on how to acquire the skills required in the examination.

***Cambridge First Certificate Practice Tests* contains:**

- six complete practice tests for the Cambridge First Certificate in English
- full information about each paper
- exam technique sections – hints and tips for the student on how to approach each paper
- hints on how to approach each of the composition question types
- extra vocabulary practice for the Use of English paper
- high quality, full colour photographs for the Speaking paper
- listening practice containing a variety of accents, recorded by professional actors
- a wide range of topics in all papers to cover all the themes likely to be encountered at this level

The first four tests in Cambridge First Certificate Practice Tests can be completed by students at home as homework and then checked in class. The last two tests can be carried out under timed conditions prior to the final examination, in order to give students a realistic expectation of the time available. It is suggested that all unknown vocabulary is given due attention in the classroom – students should be encouraged to write down the new words and expressions in their notebooks, along with any collocations or derivatives. Certain vocabulary can be selected for the students to practice, either in writing or as a basis of any spoken activities. Students who use new vocabulary in realistic activities in the classroom are more likely to retain such items and to incorporate them effectively into their spoken and written work at a later date.

Cambridge First Certificate in English (FCE): A brief outline of each paper

PAPER 1: READING (1 hour 15 minutes)

Students are asked to carry out a variety of comprehension tasks based on passages varying in length from approximately 350 to 700 words. The paper contains four parts, one of which may contain two or more shorter, related texts. There is a total of 35 questions. All answers are written in pencil on a separate answer sheet.

PAPER 2: WRITING (1 hour 30 minutes)

Two compositions to be written. The first question in Part 1 is compulsory for all candidates and includes material of up to 250 words (with the possible addition of graphic or pictorial material) that students are expected to manipulate in an appropriate manner. In Part 2, students choose one question from a range of task types, including a question on the optional set book. Compositions have to be written in blue or black pen and NOT in pencil.

Note: The set books are changed frequently and it is, therefore, unrealistic to provide specific questions related to any particular book. However, based on experience and previous examination questions, we have provided a wide range of questions that can be applied to whichever set book the student is reading and studying.

PAPER 3: USE OF ENGLISH (1 hour 15 minutes)

The paper contains five parts. Questions for Parts 1 (multiple choice cloze), 2 (open cloze), 4 (error correction) and 5 (word formation) are based on texts of approximately 100 to 300 words. Part 3 consists of 10 gapped sentences and a lead-in sentence for students to perform 'key' word transformations. There is a total of 65 questions. All answers for Part 1 are written in pencil on a separate answer sheet. Parts 2 to 5 should be completed on the separate answer sheet in INK.

PAPER 4: LISTENING (approximately 40 minutes)

A cassette recording for the four parts of the paper, each of which is heard twice. Pieces include a wide range of items that a student would be expected to encounter on a visit to an English-speaking country. Students will be expected to complete a range of comprehension tasks including multiple choice, note-taking or blank-filling, multiple matching and selecting from two or three possible answers (yes/no, true/false, etc.). Answers are marked directly on the question paper and students have five minutes at the end of the test to transfer their answers onto a separate answer sheet (Parts 1 and 3 to be completed in pencil and Parts 2 and 4 in ink).

PAPER 5: SPEAKING (approximately 15 minutes)

Students are interviewed in pairs in the presence of two examiners. One examiner takes the role of interlocutor and assessor and asks questions or provides written or spoken stimuli for the candidates. The other examiner does not contribute to the conversation but observes and assesses each candidate. There are four parts in this paper.

Part 1 Students are encouraged to give information about themselves.

Part 2 Students take turns to talk about colour photographs they are given and to comment briefly on their partner's photographs.

Part 3 Students work with each other, using visual prompts, to generate a discussion that might involve tasks such as problem solving, prioritising, etc.

Part 4 Students are invited to discuss themes related to Part 3 with each other and the interlocutor.

Marking System

The overall grade is based on the aggregate score for all five papers. In other words, if you fail one paper, it is still possible to pass. Pass grades are A, B and C. Fail grades are D and E. The results slips of students indicate areas in which a high level of performance has been achieved (for those candidates who achieve a pass grade) or where performance is particularly weak (for candidates with fail grades).

On the day of the First Certificate examination

The written parts of the exam are normally taken on the first Saturday in December or the last Saturday in May and are in the following order:

Paper 2: Writing
Paper 1: Reading
Paper 3: Use of English
Paper 4: Listening

There are short breaks between each of the papers. Although you are given a time for the Listening paper on the Statement of Entry/Timetable issued by the British Council, this time is often adjusted according to local conditions. Listen carefully when you take the Use of English paper as the invigilator will inform you then as to what time you will actually take the Listening exam. The interview (Speaking paper) may be scheduled several days before or after the date of the written exam. Full details as to where and when will be stated on the form you receive.

When you go to the examination centre, you need to take with you:

- The Statement of Entry/Timetable
- legal identification, such as a current passport or your ID card
- pencils (for use on the separate answer sheets)
- blue or black pens (for writing compositions)
- a pencil sharpener
- an eraser

Note: Students are reminded that Papers 1, 3 and 4 are scanned by a computer for marking and, therefore, use of correction fluids is not recommended.

An in-depth look

You have 1 hour 15 minutes to complete **Paper 1**: **Reading**. It tests your ability to understand written English.

The Reading paper has four parts.

Part 1
This has six or seven headings or summary sentences that have to be matched to the paragraphs in a short text. This tests an ability to read for detail and to extract the main point from a paragraph. You need to understand and recognise the topic sentence(s) within paragraphs to succeed in this part of the examination. Learning to summarise paragraphs and whole texts, in your own words, will help you to achieve the necessary skills for this task.

Part 2
This consists of a short text followed by seven or eight four-option multiple choice questions and tests your detailed comprehension of the passage. One or two questions may test whether you have understood the global meaning of the text. Learn to justify your choice before settling on a final answer. In this way, you will avoid making wild guesses or being tripped up by distractors.

Part 3
This part of the paper asks you to decide where six or seven paragraphs or sentences should be placed in the text. These will have been removed from the passage and placed at random after the text. This task is designed to test your knowledge of aspects of text structure like coherence and cohesion.

Part 4
The final part of the paper tests your ability to extract information quickly from a text without reading every single word. You will be asked to carry out a multiple matching task that contains 14 questions (on occasion, the last two questions may be multiple choice). Practice reading texts for specific information and speed up your search time by not getting stuck on unknown words or reading parts of the text that are not relevant to the question.

Marking system and answer sheet
Each correct answer for questions 1-21 is worth two marks for a total of 42 possible marks.
Each correct answer for questions 22-35 is worth one mark for a total of 14 marks.
You need to correctly answer at least 60% (ie, 37 marks out of 56) to guarantee passing this paper. The total mark is then scaled down to a mark out of 40.

You will mark your answers in pencil on a separate answer sheet, which will be scanned by computer. The test has to be completed in the time given – **extra time is not allowed for you to transfer your answers to the answer sheet**.

Exam technique

Knowing how to manage your time in the **Reading** part of the examination is just as important as being able to understand the texts and the tasks.

You have 1 hour 15 minutes to complete this paper. Each part tests different reading skills and, therefore, your time will not necessarily be evenly divided between each part. We recommend that you allow yourself approximately 15 minutes for Part 1, about 20 minutes for Part 2, 25 to 30 minutes for Part 3 and the remainder of the time (between 10 and 15 minutes) for Part 4. It is a good idea to practise timing yourself even when you are working at home. In this way, you will discover which parts of the paper are most easy or difficult for you to do.

Wear a watch to the examination room and time yourself throughout.

Answer every question. If you find yourself running out of time, it is better to guess (especially the multiple choice questions) than to leave a blank.

There is no need to rush through the paper in order to be the first one to finish! Take the appropriate time needed. If you do find that you have finished early, then go back and check your answers once or twice to make sure you haven't made any silly mistakes. However, don't change your answers unnecessarily – some students get the answer right the first time and then change the right answer to a wrong one when they are checking. If you can justify your answer sensibly to yourself, then leave it as it is – it's probably right.

Finally, you can remain calm physically and mentally by preparing properly for the exam well in advance. Make sure you understand what you have to do. Arrange to have some refreshments during the break. Check that you have several pencils, a pencil sharpener and an eraser with you for Paper 1. And, get a good night's sleep the night before the exam – last minute studying is hardly likely to help you.

Hints on answering the multiple matching section (Part 1)

Approach
Read the whole text through first. Then read each paragraph slowly, trying to get the main point. Then look down the list of headings or summary sentences and match it with the one which fits best. Do not be distracted by individual words. If you cannot match one paragraph, leave it and go on to the next one – but don't forget to come back to it. Answer all the questions. Do not panic when you come across unknown words.

Pre-exam preparation
Practise making your own headings or summary sentences from a text and be prepared to justify why you think it is a good heading or summary sentence. You can work with a partner to practise testing each other. Practise reading for gist (general meaning) and then summarising a text paragraph by paragraph for a classmate.

Remember
Pay attention to the overall theme of the paragraphs in Part 1 of the paper and don't be afraid to change your mind as you work your way through the text.

Part 1

You are going to read a newspaper article about the advantages and disadvantages of owning a racing greyhound. Choose the most suitable heading from the list **A-I** for each part (**1-7**) of the article. There is one extra heading which you do not need to use. There is an example at the beginning (**0**).

A	An expensive start
B	How to pick a champion
C	Almost the winners
D	Even winners can be losers
E	Cutting down the risk
F	A popular pastime
G	Bargains do exist
H	There's money to be made
I	An investment to get excited about

Your Money Can Live a Dog's Life

Alternative investments – the pros and cons of owning a greyhound

0 I

There must be wiser investments, but it's doubtful whether many will provide the same sort of excitement. If you're looking for financial adventure, forget your savings accounts – let your money go to the dogs.

1

Greyhound racing might be suffering from an image problem, but the dogs still have their fans. After football, it is the second biggest spectator sport in Britain. More than 70,000 races are run each year, watched by 4 million people. And more than £2 billion is spent each year on betting.

2

In the past two years, two greyhounds – *Some Picture* and *Tom's the Best* – were candidates for the BBC Sports Personality of the Year. However, in both cases the award went to a human. What a shame!

3

But there are significant financial rewards on offer if your dog turns out to be a champion. For instance, if it wins the English, Irish or Scottish Derby, you collect £50,000 in prize money. However, this is very little compared to what you can make on breeding. This can add up to total earnings in excess of £350,000 over seven years.

4

Admittedly, the chances of your picking a champion are probably only slightly better than winning the lottery and the initial stake is much higher. Even a puppy will cost you £300 and you have to rear the dog for 18 months before it is allowed to run. Rearing and schooling costs about £3 a day, so you will probably spend another £1,500 without any guarantee that the dog will be any use on the track.

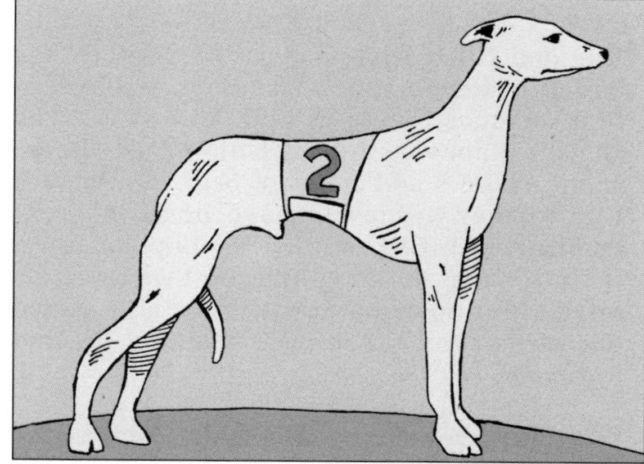

5

To avoid the uncertainty, some owners prefer to buy a dog that has proved itself and is ready to run. The cost, though, is around £3,000, even at the bottom end of the market, and some rich enthusiasts have been known to pay up to £25,000 for a promising young dog.

6

However, some of the cheaper buys are surprisingly successful. Two years ago, a dog called *Stows Val*, which had cost its owner £500, ran in the finals of the English Derby. This season a dog called *Cee Kay* bought for £1,500 has already won its owner £20,000 in prize money.

7

Even if your dog does start winning, it is unlikely that you'll be taking early retirement. Normal races at stadiums such as Walthamstow and Wimbledon net the winner no more than £50-£100, and as a greyhound usually races once every ten days or so, this isn't enough to pay for its upkeep, even if it wins regularly.

Part 2

You are going to read part of a travel article about Skiathos. For questions **8-14**, choose the answer **A**, **B**, **C** or **D** which you think fits best according to the text.

LOOKING FOR NOBODY

Dan and I flew from Gatwick to Skiathos, the busiest of the Sporades Islands, an archipelago that includes Skopelos and Alonissos. The charter plane was full of Union Jack shorts, ghetto-blasters and crates of beer. Tickets for this former hideaway have been in great demand since BBC television's popular travel show, *Holiday*, declared it the best value sun on offer. Its Koukounaries cove was also named one of the world's ten most beautiful beaches by *Conde Nast Traveller*.

When we arrived, the road builders were out in force, still surfacing the route which takes the hordes by coach from the airport to the sea. We rolled up our sleeves, put on our sunglasses and hired a motorbike. The search for seclusion began immediately.

We started with the famous Koukounaries beach, where sun-loungers were lined up four deep, the bar was churning out chips and the motor boats were screeching water skiers around the bay. There was not a spare patch of sand in sight. We walked to the end of the beach, not imagining the next cove along would be much different, but for some reason there were only two families playing in the sand. This was great, but we kept going to the next cove and suddenly, less than 100 yards from the chaos, we were alone.

Our desire for peace was satisfied by several hours of solitary swimming, but to get back to our cottage we had to go past the crowds again. So we took our motorbike and headed for the hills. A single road led to the north of the island, where our map suggested there were no big resorts, just scattered villages. The road zigzagged above lush forests, the breeze bringing with it the scent of pine and the salty taste of the sea.

Suddenly the road became a dirt track and dropped towards the island's northern coast. Our £5-a-day motorbike 'phutted' nervously. The route became rougher until we were bumping along a treacherous stony path. On one side we were confronted by a sheer rock face, on the other by a huge drop. We went through bushes and splashed through muddy streams. As the journey became more and more risky, I began to think that populated beaches were not so bad after all.

Then the view opened up and we glimpsed a huge, empty bay with a single tiny shack at one end. When we eventually reached the hut – a small taverna – its owner emerged yawning from a backroom siesta, explaining that he hadn't expected anyone to turn up at lunchtime.

The grey pebble beach, surrounded by wild flowers, is called Kehrias, and its tiny taverna is famous for bubbly cheese omelettes. Tucking into the speciality dish, we gazed at the surroundings – no cold beer here, just a few rusty outboard motors, fishing nets and a mirror surrounded by driftwood. Most people arrive by sea, the owner explained – only the English turn up by road. So we decided to hire a boat.

On the island's northern extremes – unreachable by road – we found Lalaria, a spectacular bay with no sound, just smooth white pebbles and crystal waters sparkling with blue-grey fish. At one end a giant arch of rock stuck out of the coast, under which a shoal was hanging, eerily still, in the shade. Sitting in the sun, staring out to sea, we thought we had probably found the most secluded place on Skiathos.

8 What conclusion can be reached in the first paragraph?

A Only British tourists visit Skiathos.
B Skiathos has always been very popular with tourists.
C People are greatly influenced by television.
D *Conde Nast Traveller* is read widely in Europe.

9 How could Koukounaries beach best be described?

A strange
B overcrowded
C peaceful
D traditional

10 Why did they use their motorbike to return to the cottage?

A to explore the island
B to see how good it was
C to avoid other tourists
D to get back more quickly

11 Why did the writer 'begin to think that populated beaches were not so bad after all'(line 45)?

A She was frightened.
B She felt lonely.
C She wanted to find a sandy beach.
D She wanted to do some water-skiing.

12 What did the owner do when they arrived at the taverna?

A He gave them a warm welcome.
B He offered them a cold beer.
C He told them he was about to have a nap.
D He prepared lunch for them.

13 What did the taverna owner say to the writer?

A English people hardly ever visited Kehrias beach.
B He could rent them a boat cheaply.
C Most people reached Kehrias beach by boat.
D He expected to be very busy that evening.

14 What did the couple do at Lalaria Bay?

A They sat in the shade.
B They sunbathed on the white sand.
C They did some fishing.
D They enjoyed the peace and quiet.

Part 3

You are going to read the last in a series of articles about a person who had eye surgery. Choose from the sentences **A-I** the one which fits each gap (**15-21**). There is an example at the beginning (**0**).

I can see clearly now

My appointment was on a Saturday at 10 am. My left eye was to be treated first because its vision was slightly worse. In the waiting room, I struck up a conversation with a woman who told me that it was her second attempt at surgery. **0** I Just what I wanted to hear.

Before I went into the operating theatre, I was given anaesthetic eye drops and some tablets to take the edge off my nerves. **15** ____ This was an advantage because the doctor was able to talk me through the procedure so I knew exactly what was to come.

Lying flat on my back, I was told to look at the red light above me. I was given more anaesthetic drops and then a clamp was fixed onto my face to keep my eyelids apart. **16** ____

The flap, which looked just like cling film, was then peeled back, leaving a 'trap door' for the laser. After the beam had worked its magic, the corneal flap was smoothed back in place. **17** ____ The only pain I felt was from the pressure of the clamp, but that quickly wore off.

Half an hour later, I had a check-up and, in that short time, the vision in my left eye had improved tenfold. It was incredible. After the check-up, I was told to come back for another the next morning. **18** ____ I was absolutely ecstatic.

19 ____ The following Monday I was back at work. To prevent infection, I was given antibiotic eye drops and advised to avoid eye make-up and activities such as swimming and gardening for about a week.

A month later, I had my right eye treated. Things didn't go as well this time round and I was left with a slight blurring, which has never really gone away. **20** ____ The doctor said that if it really bothered me, it could be corrected with further laser treatment.

After thinking about it for a few weeks, I decided against another operation. **21** ____ To be honest, the blurring doesn't matter at all. My vision is perfect when I use both eyes and it is wonderful not to have to bother with lenses or glasses any more.

A The post-op check-up the following morning went smoothly.

B I didn't want to risk more surgery.

C It was all over in fifteen minutes.

D I was conscious throughout the surgery.

E Next a suction ring was placed over my eye to secure it while an instrument called a microkeratone cut a flap in my cornea.

F It's barely noticeable, but after the amazing success of the first operation, I felt disappointed.

G While I waited for an appointment with a leading ophthalmologist, the operation was all I could think about.

H On the way home, I kept testing my vision by covering my right eye and reading street signs and car number plates.

I Apparently, the first time there was a complication which meant that the procedure had to be stopped and postponed for three months.

Part 4

You are going to read some information about winter holiday destinations. For questions **22-35**, choose from the list of destinations (**A-F**). The destinations may be chosen more than once. When more than one answer is required, these may be given in any order. There is an example at the beginning (**0**).

At which holiday destination(s)

might you expect something worse than you actually get?	**0** E	
are the locals particularly hospitable?	**22**	
would you find the pace of life slow?	**23**	**24**
has there been a great increase in the tourist industry?	**25**	
would you see ultra modern buildings?	**26**	
could you choose between exciting nightlife and a relaxing holiday?	**27**	
could you eat particularly good food?	**28**	
would you see a relatively old means of transport	**29**	
could you play a sport?	**30**	
would you not see large numbers of tourists?	**31**	
would you see buildings which you could see in other countries?	**32**	
have there been great changes in the recent past?	**33**	**34**
could you travel along waterways?	**35**	

Winter Blues

Leave the gloom and head for warmer climes.
Four million Britons take their holidays at this time of the year, so why not join them?

A The British Virgin Islands

More than 50 tiny volcanic islands make up the British Virgin Islands which are popular with experienced Caribbean travellers because they have escaped the problems created by mass tourism. This is the Caribbean you dream of: green, tropical islands fringed by golden beaches and populated by easygoing, relaxed people. The Sugar Mill on Tortola, the main island, is set in a 17th Century sugar plantation on a hillside. This quiet hotel is renowned for its award-winning restaurant.

B Cuba

The American trade embargo has left Cuba in a time warp. Recent investment in tourism has brought a surge of visitors – Cuba was the fastest-growing destination last winter. Tours of the colonial cities can be added to packages in all-inclusive beach resorts, although more recent history has its own appeal – the battered 1950s cars, for example.

C Dubai

After a decade of remarkable architectural development, Dubai, the most progressive city in the Arab world, is a place for the 21st Century, with futuristic buildings spreading out from the traditional Gulf port. You can shop in a souk, play golf on immaculate oasis-like courses and enjoy four-wheel adventures in the desert. The flight time from London is only six hours on Emirates, rated the best airline for the past three years. The new Ritz-Carlton Dubai, built in Mediterranean style on Jumerah beach is perfect for travellers who enjoy a touch of luxury.

D Kerala

The state of Kerala on India's south-west coast has a rich, cosmopolitan history with Chinese, Portuguese, Jewish, Dutch and Hindu influences reflected in the architecture, food, music and people. This is the most gentle corner of India with an unhurried pace. Watch the fishers on Cochin or explore backwater canals by boat. Kerala is also home to the ancient art of Ayurvedic healing.

E Benidorm

Don't be put off by Benidorm's rapid rise from fishing village to concrete holiday resort in the 1960s. It was the first Spanish resort to be 'rebuilt'. The town has been improved considerably with the worst of the early buildings being pulled down. The main beaches are meticulously maintained and the water is clean. There are cafés serving full English breakfasts as well as tapas bars. Don't expect solitude.

F Cyprus

The Greek Cypriots offer as warm a welcome as the weather. The big resorts are ideal for those who want beaches and evening activity, but for every concrete corner of Cyprus there are green mountains and pine forests, fortresses and ruins in a biblical landscape. For a taste of local atmosphere, stay in a small village inn.

An in-depth look

You have 1 hour 30 minutes to complete **Paper 2: Writing**. During this time you have to complete two tasks. In Part 1 the task is compulsory – all candidates have to answer this question, which is a formal/informal transactional letter. In Part 2 you write one of a choice of tasks that may include an article, a report, an informal (non-transactional) letter, a discursive composition, a narrative, a descriptive composition, a short story or a choice of two options based on the optional set book.

Students should be able to write in an appropriate style, using relevant vocabulary, for the particular task they choose.

There are 20 marks for each piece of work and students who pass are able to produce writing that is organised, interesting, takes into account the expectations of the target reader, and includes appropriate vocabulary and expressions with the required register and format.

You answer the questions on the lined paper provided by the examination centre. You must write in blue or black pen and NOT in pencil.

Exam technique

You have 1 hour 30 minutes to write two compositions. This gives you plenty of time for planning, writing and checking, but you still need to pay attention to time to make sure you give equal time to both tasks. Doing a good job on one task and rushing the other will not give you the best result.

Some students think that planning is a waste of time and usually panic because they think they don't have enough time to write. However, the average person can write at a speed of 25 words per minute (longhand), which means that to write between 120 and 180 words you would need around 5 to 8 minutes to complete one composition.

Spend about 5 minutes reading the questions and understanding them before you make your choice. Part 1 is a compulsory task, but in Part 2 you can choose a topic that you can do well at. Don't choose something unusual just to be clever. It is better to choose something that you are comfortable with, where you can express yourself using a wide range of vocabulary and expressions.

Take about 10 minutes to plan each composition: write down the first ideas that come to mind and then order them into paragraphs. Check that you have covered all the points that are mentioned in the question.

You should spend about 20 to 25 minutes writing each composition. You will then have about 10 minutes left to check both compositions for careless mistakes in spelling, vocabulary or grammar. Make sure you write the correct number of words. Compositions that are too short or too long will not receive the best mark.

Take two or three pens with you and make sure your writing is clear.

Hints on writing a transactional letter

One of the most important things to remember when doing this question is to read all the information given to you very carefully. Understand what exactly you have to do. You must write a formal or informal transactional letter. This tests an ability to use the usual conventions of letter writing ('Dear Sir', etc.) and to organise a letter in a sound, structured manner. It is also a test to see if you can elicit the appropriate information from the material given to you to achieve the task set.

The types of transactional letter you are likely to come across are:

- asking for or giving information
- recommending something to somebody
- giving advice or your opinion
- apologising
- giving instructions or directions
- inviting
- complaining
- applying for a job

You may find that the letter you are asked to write combines two of the above types. Whatever the case, you should be able to write in an appropriate style.

Approach

Make sure your letter is properly structured and that you cover all the points given in the question. If all the points have not been covered you will lose marks. Do not simply make a list of questions or statements in the letter. Your letter must be clearly laid out with the appropriate language (formal or informal, etc.). If you are required to ask for information, don't ask in the same way for every item. You should provide evidence of a range of language. For example, don't use 'Could you tell me ...' all the time, but use 'I would like to know ...', etc. so that the letter does not become too repetitive. Remember Dear Sir/Madam – Yours faithfully and Dear Mr/Ms – Yours sincerely. You can add an extra question of your own if you wish. This will show the examiner that you fully understand the task.

Pre-exam preparation

Practise doing all types of this task. Your teacher will be able to guide you through the various types of letter required.

Remember

Don't just copy the notes given to you – you are expected to expand them and to put them in your own words where possible.

Part 1

You **must** answer this question.

1 You help to organise camping holidays for young people. You have written to an agency that specialises in this kind of holiday, asking for information about their Windermere camp site. You have just received a letter from the tour operators in reply to your enquiry.

Read the letter, on which you have made some notes, and write a reply.

Unfortunately due to circumstances beyond our control the Windermere camp site will not be open until 27th June. If you wish to re-book at a later date, please inform us of the new arrangements. If this is impossible, we have two camp sites that are similar to Windermere. Both have almost the same facilities as Windermere so they should be perfectly acceptable to your group.

I look forward to hearing from you.

Yours sincerely

John Miles

John Miles

Write a **letter** of between **120** and **180** words in an appropriate style. Do not write any addresses.

Part 2

Write an answer to **one** of the questions **2-5** in this part. Write your answer in **120-180** words in an appropriate style.

2 You have recently returned from a walking holiday. Your cousin, who lives abroad, was due to go on the holiday with you but was not able to do so. Write a letter to your cousin, describing the holiday. Describe how you spent your time, anything unusual that happened and include some details about the people you met on holiday. Do not write any addresses.

Write your **letter**.

3 You have decided to enter a short story competition. The competition rules say that the story must begin with the following words:

It was just after midday when we realised we were lost.

Write your **story** for the competition.

4 A magazine for young people has invited you to suggest helpful ways of getting rid of stress. Write an article for the magazine, giving your suggestions.

Write your **article**.

5 Background reading texts

Answer **one** of the following two questions based on your reading of **one** of the set books. Your answer should contain enough detail to make it clear to someone who may not have read the book.

Either (a) Describe one of the main characters and state why you liked or didn't like him or her. Write a composition and refer to specific incidents to support your answer.

or (b) You have been asked to recommend the book to other students by reading a particular part of it. Write a composition giving a detailed description of the part you would choose and say why you believe it would be of interest.

An in-depth look

You have 1 hour 15 minutes to complete **Paper 3**: **Use of English**. This part of the examination is in five parts.

Part 1

In this part of the test you are tested on your ability to recognise the structure and patterns of the language, with particular emphasis on lexical items that go together (collocations), standard expressions and a few grammatical points. You are given a text with 15 gaps, followed by 15 multiple choice questions, where you have to choose a correct answer from A, B, C or D.

Part 2

A short text containing 15 gaps which have to be completed with one word. This tests the student's ability to recognise grammatical elements of a text and may include such items as prepositions, standard expressions, relative pronouns, parts of tenses missing, gerunds/infinitives, elements of the passive voice, possessive pronouns, comparatives, superlatives, etc.

Part 3

This is the only part of this paper where questions are not based on a text. Instead, you are given 10 lead-in sentences, a 'key' word and part of the response. You have to complete the response using the 'key' word and up to four other words that you consider appropriate. The 'key' word must not be changed in form. In some cases, you are being tested on two items within one sentence. Although the emphasis here is on testing grammar, you may find that some of the grammar includes items that may be considered to be lexical – for example, phrasal verbs. Other items likely to be tested are modals, conditionals, transforming active to passive and direct to indirect speech, expressions that are followed by either the gerund or the infinitive, as well as manipulation of tenses (in particular the use of the present perfect simple and continuous).

Part 4

Usually a 15-line text that contains extra or unnecessary words. Some lines of the text are correct. You have to identify the errors which could be unnecessary pronouns, prepositions, articles, etc.

Part 5

The final part of this paper is a text that has 10 gaps. Each gap has to be filled using a 'base' or 'root' word which you have to transform, using appropriate prefixes, suffixes and/or changing the given word in other ways. In most cases, you are given the verb form and have to form a relevant noun or adjective. You may also be expected to provide the plural or the negative or opposite form of the word provided.

Marking system and answer sheet

Questions 1 to 30 (Parts 1 and 2) and questions 41 to 65 (Parts 4 and 5) carry one mark each. Questions 31 to 40 (Part 3) are given either one or two marks according to a pre-determined scale. Students should be careful when marking their answer sheets in this part of the exam. Part 1 should be answered in pencil (like Paper 1: Reading), Parts 2 to 5 should be completed in pen. Answer directly on your answer sheets as you are not given extra time to transfer answers.

Exam technique

We will look at each task type in detail throughout the book.

Manage your time carefully in this paper. You have 75 minutes to complete 65 questions, so there is not much time to waste.

Make sure you write your answers in the correct place on the answer sheet.

Check that you have pencils and pens for this paper as you will need to use both.

Your writing should be legible – if it's not clear you could lose marks.

Hints on answering the multiple choice cloze passage (Part 1)

You must choose one word or phrase from a set of four (**A**, **B**, **C** or **D**) to fill a gap in a text. This tests a number of items.

1 Meaning
It may involve choosing a word according to meaning only. For example:

It is common for .... to visit Delphi during the summer.

A observers **B** spectators **C** sightseers **D** passers-by

The answer is 'sightseers' because it fits in terms of meaning.

2 Grammar
It may involve choosing a word that fits in with the grammar of the sentence. For example:

He never .... in reaching the source of the river.

A managed **B** achieved **C** arranged **D** succeeded

The answer is 'succeeded', not because it is the only word that fits in with the meaning but because it is the only one that is followed by 'in' and a gerund.

3 Fixed phrase
It may involve choosing a word that fits in a set phrase. For example:

Students rarely .... any notice of their landlords.

A paid **B** took **C** got **D** brought

The answer is 'took' because it is part of the phrase 'take notice of'.

4 Collocation
It may involve choosing a word that usually goes together with another word. For example:

The .... road was once used by smugglers.

A curling **B** rolling **C** winding **D** waving

The answer is 'winding' because it is the only one that goes with 'road'.

5 Phrasal verbs
It may involve choosing a word that forms a phrasal verb, with the correct meaning. For example:

Scientists have been quick to .... out the problems with the new theory.

A point **B** give **C** let **D** come

The answer is 'point', not because the other words do not form phrasal verbs with the word 'out', but because 'point out' fits in with the meaning of the sentence.

Approach
Read the title carefully and the text as a whole to get the general idea of what it is about. You can try and guess the missing word without looking at the choices first if you want (this is not easy). Finally, bear in mind the task type before you choose your answer.

Pre-exam preparation
Read as widely as possible so that you familiarise yourself with collocations and learn whole phrases rather than individual words. Do vocabulary practice exercises that bring out the differences in meaning between similar words.

Remember
Before making your choice, read the whole sentence to make sure it makes sense!

Part 1

For questions **1-15**, read the text below and decide which answer **A**, **B**, **C** or **D** best fits each space. There is an example at the beginning (**0**).

0	**A**	tales	**B**	accounts	**C**	stories	**D**	statements

0	A	B	C	D
	▭	▭	▬	▭

SPACE-AGE DENTISTRY

Because of all the horror (0) .... associated with a visit to the dentist, there are few people who enjoy making a dentist (1) .... Sitting in a hard chair, listening to the whining noise of a drill is usually enough to (2) .... the bravest person off, even before (3) .... has begun. In addition to that, there are long needles and hazardous x-rays to (4) .... with.

All this may be (5) .... to change, though, as hi-tech equipment makes its way into the dentist's space-age (6) .... The drill will be (7) .... by a new, painless instrument that fires metal particles (8) .... the tooth in order to cut through it. NASA software will calculate the chances of tooth (9) .... and x-ray images will be provided without radiation.

The dentist's chair of the future will have significant changes (10) .... to it, too. It will be comfortable and able to warn the dentist if (11) .... become nervous by measuring their pulse. While (12) .... on the specially designed chair, they will be able to select their favourite TV show or a film to (13) .... on a personalised 3D (14) .... to help them relax. These changes will make a visit to the dentist no more painful than sitting in the waiting (15) .... itself.

1	**A**	meeting	**B**	appointment	**C**	reservation	**D**	rendezvous
2	**A**	take	**B**	put	**C**	get	**D**	send
3	**A**	therapy	**B**	cure	**C**	healing	**D**	treatment
4	**A**	cope	**B**	tolerate	**C**	face	**D**	oppose
5	**A**	certain	**B**	about	**C**	possible	**D**	ready
6	**A**	studio	**B**	office	**C**	surgery	**D**	bureau
7	**A**	exchanged	**B**	swapped	**C**	replaced	**D**	renewed
8	**A**	from	**B**	to	**C**	at	**D**	through
9	**A**	rot	**B**	decay	**C**	wear	**D**	repair
10	**A**	done	**B**	taken	**C**	put	**D**	made
11	**A**	patients	**B**	customers	**C**	clients	**D**	contacts
12	**A**	leaning	**B**	laying	**C**	stretching	**D**	lying
13	**A**	look	**B**	watch	**C**	glance	**D**	observe
14	**A**	board	**B**	frame	**C**	screen	**D**	projector
15	**A**	room	**B**	lounge	**C**	hall	**D**	office

Part 2

For questions **16-30**, read the text below and think of the word which best fits each space. Use only **one** word in each space. There is an example at the beginning (**0**).

Richard Trevithick (1771-1833)

(0) Although / While. steam engines are no (16) .... in use in most parts of the world, they have played an important part in the history of transport. The perfection of a high-pressure steam engine was achieved about two hundred years (17) .... by an Englishman (18) .... Richard Trevithick.

His father was a respected engineer in Cornwall, south-west England, where Richard (19) .... born. (20) .... a boy, Richard learned a great deal from his father before going (21) .... to become a leading engineer in Cornish mining.

When he was still (22) .... his twenties, he realised the pumping machinery in deep mines was not good (23) .... so he invented (24) .... that (25) .... be used in even the deepest tin mines. He then perfected a high-pressure steam engine which was eventually used in a road locomotive (26) .... the beginning of the nineteenth century. Later on, his idea was developed by George Stevenson, who (27) .... in building the first steam train.

(28) .... his other successful ideas were the use of iron in shipbuilding and the use of steam in agriculture. Trevithick received neither recognition (29) .... reward for his inventions. As a result, he made very (30) .... money from all his hard work.

Part 3

For questions **31-40**, complete the second sentence so that it has a similar meaning to the first sentence, using the word given. **Do not change the word given**. You must use between two and five words including the word given. There is an example at the beginning (**0**).

Example:

0 You can't use any other method.
only
This .... you can use.

The gap can be filled by the words 'is the only method' so you write:

0	*is the only method*

31 I'd rather not go out this evening.
feel
I .... out this evening.

32 There is too much light in this room for us to develop photographs.
enough
It .... in this room for us to develop photographs.

33 We hope to visit you again soon.
forward
We .... you again soon.

34 Sheila spends most of her time at home these days.
hardly
Sheila .... these days.

35 Harold couldn't give them a description of the burglar.
hard
Harold found .... the burglar.

36 I'm sure that the doctor has examined every child.
been
I'm sure that all .... by the doctor.

37 'Don't shout! I'm not deaf you know, Paula,' said her grandmother.
not
Paula's grandmother told .... she wasn't deaf.

38 Rupert began to work with Alex in 1995.
working
Rupert and Alex .... 1995.

39 Make sure you keep the receipt because Helen might want to exchange the sweater.
case
Make sure you keep the receipt .... to exchange the sweater.

40 Sarah and Peter's wedding took place last June.
got
Sarah and Peter .... June last year.

Part 4

For questions **41-55**, read the text below and look carefully at each line. Some of the lines are correct and some have a word which should not be there. If a line is correct put a tick (✓) by the number. If a line has a word which should not be there, write the word. There are two examples at the beginning (**0** and **00**).

Moving House

0	When I was about ten years old my family decided to move	**0**	✓
00	house. This did not bring them about many great changes since	**00**	*them*
41	we moved into the house next door! This may be seem rather	**41**	
42	ridiculous and, indeed, many people have said me that it is	**42**	
43	when I will tell them about it, but there was a simple	**43**	
44	explanation for the move. We moved because there was an extra	**44**	
45	bedroom in the house we moved into it, so my sister and I could	**45**	
46	each have our own room. The move itself was a great fun as	**46**	
47	the woman who had lived next door was elderly and had built	**47**	
48	up an interesting collection of old items, including records and magazines.	**48**	
49	These things, which were all piled up in the shed, were left behind	**49**	
50	when she left. The moment I saw them, I invited several of friends	**50**	
51	round to help me find out that what Mrs Roberts had 'hidden' in the	**51**	
52	shed. There were literally hundreds of LPs which we were used	**52**	
53	to throw at each other. Inevitably, they all were broken in a	**53**	
54	matter of weeks. Now, when I look back, I can't help myself wondering	**54**	
55	whether any of them were so valuable and could have been sold to a dealer.	**55**	

Part 5

For questions **56-65**, read the text below. Use the word given in capitals at the end of each line to form a word that fits in the space in the same line. There is an example at the beginning (**0**).

Racing to a Degree

For some time now (0) ....*British*......... universities have been offering new courses in	BRITAIN
addition to the (56) .... ones that previous generations could choose from.	TRADITION
The (57) .... of these is a three-year honours degree in motor sport	LATE
(58) .... and design. According to the University of Wales, which is	ENGINEER
offering the course, the (59) .... will be on the "design, analysis and	EMPHASISE
(60) .... of a competition vehicle."	OPERATE
The thirty (61) .... who have registered for the course will gain	STUDY
(62) .... experience by working as the pit crew for the University's	VALUE
own Team Darrian T90 sports car at such (63) .... circuits as	FAME
Silverstone and Brand's Hatch. Those who perform (64) .... at	FAULT
this level can look forward to (65) .... their ambition by working at	ACHIEVE
the highest level with a Formula One team.	

Vocabulary Extension

A Vocabulary Building

Complete the unfinished words in the following sentences. The words are all related to CRIME.

1 A bur........................ breaks into buildings in order to steal.

2 A pick........................ steals things from people while they are in public places.

3 The defendant's law........................ wasn't very good and he was found gu........................ by the j........................ .

4 The suspect soon conf........................ to the crime after being ar........................ by the police.

5 There wasn't enough evid........................ to con........................ the accused, so the ju........................ had no choice but to acq........................ him.

6 He was lucky to get off with a f........................ of £500 last time, but I think he'll get a prison sent........................ this time.

7 Cap........................ puni........................ still exists in many countries.

8 The ars........................ denied setting fire to the forest but an eye-wit........................ testified against him in court.

9 She'll steal from anyone; she's just a common th........................ .

10 A man in police custody has been ch........................ with mur........................ .

B Word Use

Use the words on the left to complete the sentences on the right. Make sure the word is in the correct form.

	Words		Sentences
1	**meeting** **appointment** **reservation**	a b c	She can't come to the 'phone because she's in a(n) .... I'm afraid you can't see the manager without a(n) .... Knowing how popular the restaurant was, I made a(n) ....
2	**swap** **replace** **renew**	a b c	Who's going to .... Mr Watson when he leaves? I'll have to .... my passport before I go on holiday. I wanted a window seat so I .... places with Margaret.
3	**rot** **decay** **wear**	a b c	Those boots must be good if they can stand up to so much .... and tear. We would have bought the house if there hadn't been so much dry .... Tooth .... can be avoided by good dental care.
4	**lean** **lay** **lie**	a b c	I felt dizzy so I had to .... down on my bed. Don't .... on the desk because it isn't very solid. Would you be kind enough to .... the table, please?
5	**room** **lounge** **hall**	a b c	Due to a delay we had to wait in the departure .... for three hours. By the time I reached the surgery, the waiting .... was full. I'll meet you in the entrance .... if it is raining.

C Use of Prepositions

Use the prepositions below to complete the sentences which follow.

at (x2) *by* *from* *in (x 2)* *up to* *with*

1 There has been considerable discussion about how to cope .... stress.
2 The government has succeeded .... providing employment opportunities for school leavers.
3 Joe, who is normally very talkative, remained surprisingly silent .... the beginning of the meeting.
4 Sheila published three novels while she was .... her thirties.
5 Jack's mother made him face .... his responsibilities.
6 My lawyer glanced .... his watch and said he had to ring another client.
7 This board game can be played .... people of all ages.
8 She made a lot of money .... her autobiography.

D Word Formation

I Use the word in capitals at the end of each sentence to form a word that fits in the space in the sentence.

1	He didn't make one mistake in the performance: it was	FAULT
2	Being .... challenged, he has to get around in a wheelchair.	PHYSICS
3	A course in chemical .... sounds interesting.	ENGINEER
4	.... holiday resorts are popular with the British.	SPAIN
5	I'm looking forward to meeting her .... cousin.	FAME

II Choose the odd word out from the following groups of words according to how they form nouns.

eg achieve employ refuse entertain

'refuse' is the odd word out because it forms its noun with the suffix '-al', while all the others change into a noun by adding the suffix '-ment'.

1	major	tend	popular	possible
2	prefer	confer	urgent	correspond
3	require	oblige	tempt	accuse
4	dark	sad	rude	long
5	honest	jealous	recover	weak

An in-depth look

The Listening paper consists of four parts each with a different task for you to complete. All recordings are heard twice. You may hear different accents, but any background noises will only be heard at the beginning or end of the piece to set the scene. Parts 1, 3 and 4 are objective tasks: either multiple choice, multiple matching or selecting from 2 or 3 possible answers (yes/no, true/false, etc.). Part 2 is a productive task where you are expected to take notes or complete information given.

Part 1

This is what is known as a 'fresh start activity'. Each extract you hear is unrelated to the previous or following one. You hear a series of monologues or exchanges between one or more speakers lasting approximately half a minute.

Part 2

A recording of about 3 minutes from which you have to take notes or fill in blanks. This part of the test could be either a monologue or text involving interacting speakers.

Part 3

You will hear five individual speakers or five exchanges between interacting speakers, each for about half a minute, speaking about a related topic. You have to match the speakers to a list of prompts.

Part 4

The final recording will be either a monologue or interacting speakers talking for about 3 minutes.

One mark is awarded for each correct answer through all parts of the paper. Marks are adjusted to give a mark out of 40.

Exam technique

Do your best to answer the questions on the first listening. Use the repeat recording to check your answer.

Try to understand the general meaning of what each speaker is saying, without focusing on any unknown words.

Don't panic. You have time to read the questions carefully before you hear the recording. In Part 1, the questions are also recorded, so you have plenty of time to understand what you are being asked to do.

You are given time to transfer your answers to a special answer sheet at the end of the test. Make sure you transfer your answers accurately – check that you haven't put an answer in the wrong place.

Hints on answering the multiple choice questions (Part 1)

You must answer eight multiple choice questions of three options each. The eight extracts you hear are unrelated. This item tests and focuses on an understanding of general meaning, main points, detail, location, relationships, mood, attitude, intention, feeling or opinion.

Approach
You are given time to read the multiple choice questions before you listen the first time. Make good use of this time. Answer the questions the first time you listen and check your answers during the second listening. You should justify your answers to yourself while listening the second time.

Pre-exam preparation
Listen to short extracts of speech on the radio or on TV and concentrate on understanding the main points or general idea of what you hear.

Remember
If you find one extract too difficult, don't worry. Treat each extract as a separate item and don't get stuck on one question – they are not related!

Part 1

You will hear people talking in eight different situations. For questions **1-8**, choose the best answer, **A**, **B** or **C**.

1 You hear two people talking in a café. What has the man been watching?

A a game of chess
B a basketball match
C a game of tennis

1

2 Listen to this news flash on a local radio station. What does the reporter say?

A Some people were killed in the explosion.
B The explosion was caused by a gas leak.
C Another news flash will be broadcast as soon as possible.

2

3 You hear two students talking about a lecturer. What do they say about him?

A He's very tolerant.
B He gives his students too much work.
C He makes his lectures enjoyable.

3

4 You hear a woman talking about her job. What does she do?

A She is a builder.
B She is a nurse.
C She is an engineer.

4

5 You hear two people discussing a newspaper article. What do they think about it?

A It is amusing.
B It is unfair.
C It is sad.

5

6 You hear someone talking about a holiday. What was it like?

A marvellous
B boring
C disappointing

6

7 You hear a couple having a discussion outside a pet shop. What kind of pet does the man want?

A a parrot
B a dog
C a rabbit

7

8 You hear a recording on your telephone answering machine. What does your friend want you to do?

A meet him at a hospital
B meet him at 7.30 instead of 8.00
C let him know if there is a problem with the new arrangements

8

Part 2

You will hear a radio interview with a writer. For questions **9-18**, complete the sentences. You will need to write a word or a short phrase in each box.

Dr Alan Knight's new book is called [**9**]

It has caused many readers to become [**10**]

Dr Knight works as an [**11**]

He says that flights from London to New York will take a little longer than [**12**] minutes.

He also says that trains will travel on a [**13**] field.

The population in 2020 will reach [**14**]

Some buildings will have the same facilities as a [**15**]

In 2020 people may not eat food but [**16**] instead.

These will contain all the required [**17**]

We will be able to operate machines by [**18**] to them.

Part 3

You will hear five different people talking about the biggest mistake they have made. For questions **19-23**, choose which of the people **A-F** is speaking. Use the letters only once. There is one extra letter which you do not need to use.

A	She didn't expect to be found out.			
B	She made a mistake while she was abroad.	Speaker 1		**19**
C	She still hates to admit she made a mistake.	Speaker 2		**20**
D	She gave some poor financial advice.	Speaker 3		**21**
E	She was betrayed by someone she trusted.	Speaker 4		**22**
F	She might have had a better career.	Speaker 5		**23**

Part 4

You will hear part of an interview with Michael Jones, a dealer in memorabilia. For questions **24-30**, decide whether the statements are true or false and mark **T** for True, or **F** for False.

24 Most Beatles' collectors are interested in making money. **24**

25 The prices of most Beatles' memorabilia are three times what they were five years ago. **25**

26 Nowadays there are very few old posters left. **26**

27 The Munich poster was sold for twice as much as expected. **27**

28 There are so many fake signatures because the Beatles did not want to spend so much time signing photos. **28**

29 The guitar that was offered to a dealer had a fake serial number on it. **29**

30 The Beatles' musical instruments usually fetch the highest prices. **30**

An in-depth look

You will be interviewed with another candidate for about 15 minutes and you will be assessed throughout the interview according to four analytical criteria:

- grammar and vocabulary
- discourse management
- pronunciation
- interactive communication.

In the first part of the listening paper you will be introduced to the other candidate, to the interlocutor and the assessor. You will be asked personal questions that will help with this introduction. These questions form part of the examination.

Then the examiner will use photographs to allow you to speak for an extended period of time. You will be expected to compare and contrast the photos and to give information or express your opinion. You will also be expected to respond to a question about the photos that are given to your partner in the exam.

In the third part of the exam, you will be expected to have a natural conversation with the other candidate and you will be given a task to carry out that will involve you exchanging information, expressing attitudes and opinions.

The final part of the exam is related to Part 3 in theme and you will be expected to speak to both the interlocutor and the other candidate.

Exam technique

One of the easiest ways to improve your level of spoken language is to take every opportunity you can to speak in English. Actively seek out foreigners living in your area to practice your English – don't forget that many people speak English (not just people who come from the UK or the USA). If your teacher is a native speaker of the language, then make an effort to speak to him/her as much as you can.

You can only be assessed if you open your mouth and speak. The examiner will understand if you are a little nervous, but you won't get many marks if you give just one-word answers. You are expected to use the normal conventions of continuing a conversation that you would use in your own language. Think about how you speak to your friends or parents!

The photographs are there to help you express yourself. You are not expected to describe them in great detail.

When working with your partner in Part 3, do your best to encourage him/her to speak and remember that you should reach a conclusion between you.

Hints on answering personal questions (Part 1)

You must give some personal information about yourself according to questions asked by the interlocutor (the person interviewing you).

Approach
There are no tricks here! The interlocutor requires natural answers such as those you would give when you meet a person from abroad for the first time.

Pre-exam preparation
Practise talking about yourself, your life, your likes and dislikes, your family, your hopes for the future and your studies to as many native speakers as you can find!.

Remember
The examiner is NOT interested in whether you are telling the truth. Even if you are the most boring person in the world, invent something to give an appropiate answer!

Part 1 (about 3 minutes)

Ask and answer the following questions with a partner.

- Where do you live?
- How long have you lived there?
- What's the place like?
- What do you think of it?
- What is there for people of your age to do there?

Part 2 (about 4 minutes)

Practise speaking about the photographs. Photographs for this test will be found on page 178.

Candidate A, here are your two photographs. They show animals in different situations. Please let Candidate B have a look at them. Candidate A, I'd like you to compare and contrast these photographs, saying what you think about the situation the animals are in (approximately 1 minute).

Candidate B, could you please tell us which animal you believe is happier (approximately 20 seconds).

Candidate B, here are your two photographs. They show different sports. Please let Candidate A have a look at them. Candidate B, I'd like you to compare and contrast these two photographs, saying what you think are the differences between individual sports and team sports (approximately one minute).

Candidate A, could you please tell us whether you think it is easier to play a sport on your own or in a team (approximately 20 seconds).

Part 3 (about 3 minutes)

Discuss the following with a partner.

Imagine you help to organise adventure weekends and have been asked to introduce three more activities to the programme. Talk to each other about which three activities you would choose from those shown on the opposite page and say why you think they would be appropriate. It is not necessary to agree with each other

Part 4 (about 4 minutes)

Give each other your opinions about the following questions.

- What is the best way to learn how to play a sport or game?
- What problems might someone face while learning?
- What kind of person should a sports coach be?
- What kind of person is good at sport?
- How can a sport or game help a person in life?

Hints on answering the multiple choice section (Part 2)

You must read a text and answer seven or eight multiple choice questions of four options each. This tests detailed understanding, global understanding, inference (eg What does the writer mean ...?) and lexical reference (eg What does 'it' refer to in line X?).

Approach
Do not panic when you come across unknown words. You can often guess the meaning of a word in the context of the sentence. In other cases, the meaning of an unknown word would not affect your understanding of the sentence or passage, as in Part 2 of this test, where you will find the sentence "I followed its progress with an avuncular smile." You would not be expected to understand the meaning of 'avuncular'. Read the passage through thoroughly. Do not be distracted by the incorrect answers. Remember, the correct answer comes from the text and not what you might know about the subject, so you should justify your answers to yourself before selecting your final answer. Answer all the questions.

Pre-exam preparation
Read as widely as possible. You may find that another person's strategy for doing this part of the paper does not suit you, so practise and find your best way of doing it.

Remember
If one of the questions is an incomplete sentence, your choice should match the context of the passage to give a correct answer. Other options may make complete sentences, but the information may not be relevant to the text.

Part 1

You are going to read a newspaper article about a spaceship. Choose the most suitable heading from the list **A-I** for each part (**1-7**) of the article. There is one extra heading which you do not need to use. There is an example at the beginning (**0**).

A	Burn it up
B	Nuclear protest
C	It only takes a slight error
D	Building up speed
E	Very little risk
F	A disastrous collision
G	The end of the world
H	Convincing the world
I	A change of course

Poison Spaceship May Fall to Earth

By our Science Editor

0 I

It took six years to construct and involved hundreds of scientists across America and Europe. But now activists want the six-tonne Cassini probe, currently hurtling towards Earth on its way to Saturn, to be redirected into the Sun.

1

They say the robot spaceship, which has a plutonium reactor on board, could crash as it comes within 11,000 kilometres of Earth. 'If control is lost during the fly-by, the craft would plunge into the atmosphere and its radioactive load could scatter widely,' said Najmedin Meshkakati, a professor of engineering at the University of Southern California.

2

He and other campaigners are pressing American and European politicians and space officials to have Cassini directed away from Earth. Many believe that the best solution would be to divert it into the Sun so that it would be fried to a crisp.

3

This has alarmed the European Space Agency so much that it has scheduled emergency meetings for scientists, civil servants and government press officers from its 14 member states. They will take advice on how to defend the mission: to explain the plutonium reactor and reassure the public it poses no danger.

4

To reach Saturn, the spaceship has to be flown through the solar system. It has already whipped close to Venus, a manoeuvre that gained valuable momentum. It will fly past Venus again, passing Earth two months later. Each fly-by increases momentum until it achieves the 67,000 kph needed to reach Saturn.

5

Previous probes have been sent on spirals across the solar system before heading to outer planets. However, Cassini has attracted opposition because it is carrying the heaviest nuclear reactor ever put on an interplanetary probe.

6

A fractional miscalculation during the Venus fly-by could send it plunging into our planet. And should 33 kg of plutonium spill into the atmosphere, the effects would be apparent for generations to come.

7

But NASA and European officials reject this. 'There is less than a one in a million chance of an inadvertent re-entry,' said a NASA spokesperson. And if an accident did occur, Cassini's plutonium is stored in a ceramic case which would withstand atmospheric burn-up, say scientists.

Part 2

You are going to read a newspaper article about a problem with a rat. For questions **8-14**, choose the answer **A**, **B**, **C** or **D** which you think fits best according to the text.

Who Will Rid Me of This Rat?

When I first saw it, I thought it was a squirrel. It was brown and furry and was scurrying across the garden with what looked like a nut in its mouth. I followed its progress with an avuncular smile. I am fond of squirrels: they make a nice adornment to the garden. Then I noticed the tail. Squirrels have bushy tails. This tail was pencil thin. The conclusion was alarming, but unavoidable. There was a rat on the premises.

My first instinct was to seize a broom and rush down the garden after it. It was a bad idea. The rat showed me a clean pair of heels, going from 0 to 60 in three-and-a-half seconds, and disappeared under the garden shed. Simultaneously, my next door neighbour poked her head out of her bathroom window.

'Don't do that,' she cried. 'It's cruel.' My jaw dropped in disbelief. Of all the neighbours on the planet, I had to end up with one who opposed capital punishment for rats. I slunk back into the house, feeling like a common axe murderer, and looked up *Pest Control* in the *Yellow Pages*. There had to be some quick and easy solution. After all, this was not the 1930s.

My optimism was short-lived. Two months after its first sighting, the rat is still there. It shows no signs of wanting to leave – quite the contrary. Its main residence is under the shed, but it also keeps some sort of *pied-à-terre* by the dustbin. It swaggers around the garden as if it owns the place. Perhaps it has plans to start a family. Or perhaps my neighbour is feeding it bowls of milk on the sly. I am not sure.

All I do know is that it has successfully resisted all efforts to capture it – and that, worryingly, every expert in pest control has different advice to offer.

I have found myself in a strange twilight world inhabited by men who talk in whispers and announce they will arrive in unmarked vans. They all promise results, but do not stay around long enough to deliver them.

'A bit of chicken tikka masala should do the trick,' said the man from the environmental health department. I duly visited the local Indian takeaway and kept the leftovers. Every night for a fortnight, I smeared a rat-trap with curry and, every night for a fortnight the rat ignored the bait.

'Try chocolate,' said someone else. 'Rats love chocolate.' I tried chocolate. The rat ignored that, too. I tried bread. I tried boiled sweets. I tried peanut butter. No good. My friend is a picky eater. He probably only goes into traps baited with wild salmon.

Opinion was also divided as to the best sort of trap to use. The man from the environmental health favoured a humane trap, like a walk-in wardrobe: the idea was that the rat would be captured alive and then drowned in a bucket of water. Others recommended the sort of old-fashioned traps that snapped shut and decapitated their victims. 'I wouldn't have anything to do with those humane traps,' said one expert. 'Suppose the rat has Weil's disease, you'd be dead before the week was out.' I took this advice, but to no avail.

Another suggestion came from a friend who had spent his childhood in Yorkshire. 'Get an airgun,' he said. 'You're bound to hit it, eventually.'

The most worrying aspect of the situation is that I am not alone in my plight. Two different pest control companies have told me that they have never sold so many rat traps. Rodent young are normally killed off by the cold, but the mild winter has allowed them to survive.

My rat friend has not got so cocky that he has taken to hanging around outside my study window, taking his lunch on the patio. I could kill the little pest – except that I cannot, for the life of me, work out how. Is there anybody there who can help?

8 When did the writer first realise the animal was a rat?

- **A** When he realised it wasn't carrying a nut.
- **B** When it ran into the garden.
- **C** When he saw how fast it was.
- **D** When he saw its thin tail.

9 How did the writer react to his neighbour's comment?

- **A** He became violent.
- **B** He was very surprised.
- **C** He was frightened.
- **D** He wanted to punish her.

10 What did the writer infer from the rat's behaviour after two months?

- **A** The rat was terrified of coming out into the garden.
- **B** The rat was stealing food from his house.
- **C** The rat had become more cunning.
- **D** The rat was determined to stay.

11 Why did the writer 'think' the rat avoided the traps?

- **A** The traps were in the wrong places.
- **B** The rat had expensive tastes.
- **C** He hadn't taken professional advice.
- **D** The rat was too stupid to find the food.

12 Why was the writer advised to use a trap which would kill the rat?

- **A** It might be fatal to use another kind.
- **B** It would be easier to use.
- **C** It would be more likely to produce results.
- **D** The rat might escape from another kind.

13 How does the writer feel now?

- **A** optimistic
- **B** embarrassed
- **C** desperate
- **D** sad

14 How could the article best be described?

- **A** serious
- **B** informative
- **C** amusing
- **D** instructive

Part 3

You are going to read an article about boiling vegetables. Eight sentences have been removed from the article. Choose from the sentences **A-I** the one which fits each gap (**15-21**). There is one extra sentence which you do not need to use. There is an example at the beginning (**0**).

The Truth About Over-boiled Vegetables

The truth has finally emerged. **0** I This news, which is now official, will bring great joy to thousands of retired school chefs - that fine body of men and women, whose uncompromising approach to food shaped our childhoods.

They boiled their lives away in kitchens that rattled with simmering pots. **15** ______ They boiled everything and they boiled it for ever.

It was not only in schools that the great vegetable-boilers practised their art. **16** ______ In some parts of England, no family was without one. The stove was controlled by a sweating mother who stuck a fork into the broccoli obsessively until it met no resistance.

Until last week, it was fashionable to make fun of those fine men and women. **17** ______ I remember switching on the television a couple of years ago and having to listen to a lecture by Delia Smith on the dangers of overcooked vegetables. She made me feel like a criminal.

I am not very fond of vegetables. **18** ______ Soggy carrots are horrible, but at least you can force them down your throat. Undercooked, semi-raw carrots are far worse. They set your teeth on edge and are difficult to swallow.

The tide of fashion has turned so decisively in favour of lightly boiled vegetables or, better still, braised or roasted ones that there is no point in going against it. Mushy peas have been replaced by chargrilled aubergines and you cannot get soggy cabbage in a restaurant for love or money. **19** ______

According to a Europe-wide study coordinated by the Institute of Food Research in Norwich, a well-cooked carrot offers more protection against heart disease and cancer than a raw one. **20** ______ The same is true of other vegetables.

21 ______ As for the braisers, roasters, chargrillers, steamers and poachers, they will just have to re-think their strategy.

A They had cooked all the goodness out of the vegetables – or that was the conventional wisdom.

B But the one thing I demand of a vegetable I am going to eat is that it should have been properly cooked.

C If you boil a carrot thoroughly, your body will absorb far more carotenoids, or antioxidants, which make them so healthy.

D When the cabbage was cooking, you could not see them for the clouds of steam.

E Escoffier hints that this is not how he would cook vegetables himself.

F The Army catering corps had some notable ones and so did British Rail.

G But now science, not for the first time, has come to our rescue.

H So let the nation's boilers come out and do what they do best.

I Soggy vegetables are good for you.

Part 4

You are going to read some people's opinions about why English sport is not as good as it should be. For questions **22-35**, choose from the people (**A-F**). The people may be chosen more than once. When more than one answer is required, these may be given in any order. There is an example at the beginning (**0**).

Which of the people A-F say(s) that

they can't assume we should automatically win?	**0** A	
they're doing the right things in football?	**22**	
people will face danger for financial rewards?	**23**	
in other countries players concentrate wholly on their sport?	**24**	
nowadays children have more things to do?	**25**	
they should concentrate on building a great national team?	**26**	**27**
there is no longer any pride associated with winning for England?	**28**	
other countries have become better than us?	**29**	**30**
there is plenty of money available?	**31**	
people will not give up their free time without being paid?	**32**	**33**
they are too impatient to wait for good results?	**34**	
their expectations are often too great?	**35**	

What's wrong?

Sporting figures from the past give their verdict

A David Lloyd

We have no special right to win, especially now that opposing countries have improved themselves in all sports. In cricket, for the majority of other countries, it is a way of life, but in England it is only a part of life. The methods and system we have are second to none, but we haven't got the talent or technique. In order to improve English cricket, everything has to be done with the national side in mind, as it is in Australia.

B Gary Lineker

Well, we haven't been much good at cricket for 20 years. It's fairly obvious that the sport isn't played as much in schools; it's really only played in public schools nowadays. The selling-off of playing fields didn't exactly help and teachers aren't as willing to give up their own time without proper financial rewards. As for football, I think it's heading in the right direction – we've just had a couple of bad weeks. I think we're still one of the world's top sporting nations, but we just tend to expect too much from our sportsmen and women at times.

C Dave Moorcraft

A real problem is with our schoolchildren. Two or three decades ago, we had an army of people who, for nothing, gave up their time to help kids in sport. From that resource children developed. Now the curriculum has changed and, on top of that, there are a huge number of different attractions competing for kids' attention. We cannot afford to get it wrong in schools.

D Frank Dick

We could do something very special in sport. Lottery money is pouring in, the right youngsters and the right coaches are out there. The problem is with the administration. You need to establish your aims and get the right structure to achieve them. In football, we would say that the goal is to win the World Cup. But if our priority is at club level, we can't expect results in the national team.

E Fatima Whitbread

My era was the last, I think, when we could say we were proud to hear the national anthem play after we'd won gold. That's what it was all about and it should be still. Nowadays the motivation is for money rather than achieving for your country. People will put themselves at risk and compete for money when they're not fully fit, instead of waiting until they're ready to compete.

F Roger Uttley

It's like the industrial revolution. We led the world, but then sat back and allowed the rest of the world to overtake us. When I was at school, a huge amount of work was done working with youngsters. That's not the case nowadays and that is why the number of children we used to be able to choose from is not the same. I think we also expect results immediately. This brings too much pressure which, over a period of time, can cause a lack of enthusiasm.

Hints on writing an informal/non-transactional letter

Question 2 in Part 2 of this test is an example of an informal, non-transactional letter. This type of letter would always be written for a known reader, and would be intended to interest the reader, share an experience or explain feelings or opinions.

Before writing your letter, check what items you have to include. In this case you have to give advice and make suggestions.

An effective way of making notes for your composition is to ask yourself questions and write down the answers. Here are some example questions for question 2:

What advice do I have to give? (Your answer would be 'Which clothes to bring and not to bring')
What suggestions do I have? (Your answer would come under two headings: 'Places to Visit' and 'Things to Do'.)

When you have briefly answered your questions, you are ready to add more details. For example, "It's a good idea to bring a warm jacket and don't forget your umbrella." You can then extend this by giving a reason for your choice. "When you arrive it will be the middle of winter for us and so you should expect a lot of rain." These ideas can be combined and re-worded for the final version of your composition.

Once you have all your ideas, you then need to organise them. In addition, you should think about your introductory paragraph. In this case, you might want to thank your pen friend for his or her letter.

Finally, you need to think about a suitable close to the letter. If you are going to be meeting during the visit, you could say something like "I look forward to showing you around the science museum."

How are you going to sign off? You are writing to a friend, so you won't end with 'Yours sincerely', will you? Don't forget – marks are awarded for appropriateness.

Part 1

You **must** answer this question.

1 You are a student at a college in Britain. You have seen an advertisement for a summer job which you are interested in. Read the advertisement and the notes you have made and write a letter to Ms McDonald.

Sales Assistants Required for the Summer

Due to our recent expansion programme we now have branches in several European countries, including Greece, Portugal and Spain. We are looking for energetic young sales staff to work in our stores from July to September. We offer

- a good basic salary — *how much? how many hours a week?*
- bonuses — *what for?* — and overtime — *when?*
- excellent working conditions
- generous discounts — *what do they sell?* — for staff

If you are interested, write to Ms Fiona McDonald, giving details of your previous work experience, languages spoken and reasons why we should employ you.

Barker & Webster, Ramille House, Ramille Street, London W1V 2EL

Write a letter of between **120** and **180** words in an appropriate style. Do not write any addresses.

Part 2

Write an answer to **one** of the questions **2-5** in this part. Write your answer in **120-180** words in an appropriate style.

2 Your English pen friend wants to visit your country and has written to you for advice and information. Write a letter to your pen friend, giving advice about what clothes to bring and what to avoid. You should also tell him or her about places to visit and things to do.

Write your **letter**.

3 Your teacher has asked you to write a story for the school's English language magazine. It must begin with the following words:

There was only one thing I could do.

Write your **story**.

4 You have a summer job in a cafeteria. The manager would like to make it more popular with young people and has asked you to write a report making some suggestions about what changes should be made.

Write a **report** for your manager.

5 Background reading texts

Answer **one** of the following two questions based on your reading of **one** of the set books. Your answer should contain enough detail to make it clear to someone who may not have read the book.

Either (a) A film based on the book you have read is going to be made by a local art college. As a keen amateur actor, you have been asked which character you would like to play. Write a **composition**, giving reasons for your choice.

or (b) How likely is it that the events described in the book could happen today? Write a **composition**, giving reasons for your answer.

Hints on how to gap-fill (Part 2 – cloze passage)

1 You must fill each gap in a text with a single word. This tests structure rather than vocabulary. For example:

He was brought up in London, ... he set up his business.

The missing word refers to 'London', a place – so the word that can fill the gap is 'where'.

2 There may be more than one answer, but you must only put one word on the answer sheet. For example:

The explorers realised it .... take longer than expected.

The gap can be filled by 'would, could or might' and unless the context indicates otherwise, each of these words would be correct.

Approach
Read the title and text as a whole to get an idea of what it is about. Go back through the text, filling in the most obvious words from your first reading. Look carefully at the words surrounding the gaps that are left to give you clues as to what the missing word is. Finally, read the passage all the way through to check that the words you have put in make sense and are in the correct form. Remember, spelling counts so make sure you check it carefully.

Pre-exam preparation
Learn words and expressions in context by reading as widely as possible.

Remember
If you run out of time and you really don't know the answer, then guess! At least you will have a 25% chance of getting the right answer. Blank spaces cannot earn a mark.

Part 1

For questions **1-15**, read the text below and decide which answer **A**, **B**, **C** or **D** best fits each space. There is an example at the beginning (**0**).

Example:

0 **A** freeing **B** liberating **C** escaping **D** breaking

0	A	B	C	D
	▭	▭	▬	▭

The Trachtenberg System

After (0) .... from a concentration camp in Germany during the Second World War, the late Professor Jakow Trachtenberg founded his Institute of Mathematics in Zurich. While he was a prisoner he invented a (1) .... system of mathematics which makes mathematical (2) .... much simpler, quicker and more accurate.

The Trachtenberg System is (3) .... on procedures that are quite different from those we are now (4) .... with. In order to use the system, it is only (5) .... to be able to count. The system works by using a (6) .... of rules that have to be (7) .... Once this has been done, mathematics is (8) .... a mystery, even for those who have difficulty in doing simple multiplication. The method has been successfully used by schoolchildren and university students (9) ....

In the 1950s, the system was thought to be so remarkable that many people (10) .... it would revolutionise mathematics teaching (11) .... the world. Despite the initial enthusiasm, Trachtenberg's system never really (12) .... on outside Switzerland. The (13) .... for this was probably that educators decided that learning the rules was more difficult than using traditional methods.

Nowadays, people who are (14) .... to do basic mathematics can rely on calculators or computers. Because of this, the Trachtenberg System is (15) .... to be completely forgotten in time.

1	**A** rare	**B** sole	**C** single	**D** unique
2	**A** estimates	**B** measurements	**C** calculations	**D** judgements
3	**A** relied	**B** concentrated	**C** depended	**D** based
4	**A** familiar	**B** aware	**C** used	**D** knowledgeable
5	**A** possible	**B** necessary	**C** essential	**D** required
6	**A** set	**B** group	**C** class	**D** pack
7	**A** recalled	**B** memorised	**C** reminded	**D** recollected
8	**A** no more	**B** no way	**C** no longer	**D** no further
9	**A** same	**B** like	**C** similar	**D** alike
10	**A** guessed	**B** saw	**C** predicted	**D** confirmed
11	**A** over	**B** throughout	**C** overall	**D** everywhere
12	**A** kept	**B** came	**C** brought	**D** caught
13	**A** cause	**B** reason	**C** purpose	**D** service
14	**A** incapable	**B** impossible	**C** helpless	**D** unable
15	**A** surely	**B** likely	**C** possible	**D** certainly

Part 2

For questions **16-30**, read the text below and think of the word which best fits each space. Use only one word in each space. There is an example at the beginning (**0**).

Home Video

Just (0) ....*like*................ most modern technological inventions, video cameras have improved in quality (16) .... they first became available to the public.

The video recorder was invented (17) .... Sony in 1965 and nearly a decade (18) ...., in 1974, the same company brought out the Handy Cam. This camera, which used VHS video tapes, (19) .... about £1,500. As more (20) .... more manufacturers began to make video cameras, the tapes (21) .... smaller and prices fell. Today at the end of the millennium, approximately 250,000 camcorders, which can be bought for as little as £300, (22) .... sold in the UK every year.

Even though they are popular, video cameras (23) .... not allow the person doing the filming to join in the fun. Now a solution (24) .... this problem has been found. A video camera weighing less (25) .... 90g has been developed. It can easily fit on the frame of a (26) .... of sunglasses with the recorder clipped on to a belt. It also has a special feature which prevents the picture (27) .... jumping as the wearer is moving.

This technology may have applications in the field of medicine. With (28) .... audio-video link, it will allow surgeons to carry (29) .... operations with instructions down a telephone line from a specialist (30) .... could be thousands of miles away.

Part 3

For questions **31-40**, complete the second sentence so that it has a similar meaning to the first sentence, using the word given. **Do not change the word given**. You must use between two and five words including the word given. There is an example at the beginning (**0**).

0 We have finished all the jobs.
more

There .... us to do.

The gap can be filled by the words 'are no more jobs for' so you write:

0	*are no more jobs for*

31 Shirley answered all the examination questions correctly.
mistakes

Shirley .... in the examination.

32 I haven't found a place to live yet.
still

I .... for a place to live.

33 We have never heard such a ridiculous excuse.
most

It is the .... ever heard.

34 You should always ask me if you want to borrow the car.
without

Never .... me first.

35 'Don't buy such an expensive video cassette recorder,' advised my father.
not

My father .... so much money on a video cassette recorder.

36 If you don't want any trouble, you ought to stay away from the park at night.
better

If you don't want any trouble, you .... near the park at night.

37 I want your compositions by Friday at the latest.
must

Your compositions .... by Friday at the latest.

38 Henry doesn't have enough money to live in such an expensive neighbourhood.
afford

Henry .... in such an expensive neighbourhood.

39 I don't know anything about it.
idea

I .... you're talking about.

40 She has never worked such long hours before.
used

She is .... such long hours.

Part 4

For questions **41-55**, read the text below and look carefully at each line. Some of the lines are correct and some have a word which should not be there. If a line is correct put a tick (✓) by the number. If a line has a word which should not be there, write the word. There are two examples at the beginning (**0** and **00**).

A SUMMER JOB

0 While I was a student, I used to work during the summer
00 because I needed extra money during term-time for to buy extra
41 books and to run an old car that I had. One summer I found
42 it very much difficult to find a job and was ready to give up
43 looking when a friend of mine told to me that he didn't
44 want the job his father then had managed to get for
45 him. It wasn't a particularly good type job in terms of
46 challenge or variety, but the pay it was good. The job
47 involved working nights in a pork pie factory and I decided to go
48 for an interview and a medical examination. Fortunately, I was been given
49 the job and started the following week. My shift began at six o' clock
50 in the evening and ended eight hours later, at two o' clock in the
51 following morning. There was and an opportunity to work overtime
52 from the time to time so sometimes I didn't actually get
53 to home until five or six o'clock in the morning. At first I found
54 sleeping during the day quite strange but I had soon got used to
55 it. The job had one big advantage, though. I was able to get free pork pies
whenever I wanted!

0	✓
00	for
41	
42	
43	
44	
45	
46	
47	
48	
49	
50	
51	
52	
53	
54	
55	

Part 5

For questions **56-65**, read the text below. Use the word given in capitals at the end of each line to form a word that fits in the space in the same line. There is an example at the beginning (**0**).

Helping Out

For people whose (0) ....*daily*.......... tasks present them with	DAY
difficulties due to the fact that they are (56) ...., animals,	ADVANTAGE
especially dogs, can help them regain their (57) .... by	DEPEND
performing tasks that the rest of us do (58) .... without	AUTOMATIC
giving them a second (59)	THINK
(60) .... such dogs takes about two years and the majority	TRAIN
are either poodles or gun breeds. On (61) .... of its	COMPLETE
(62) .... , the dog is able to respond to over one hundred	EDUCATE
commands which cater for its new owner's (63) .... needs.	BASE
After that, the dog can be taught any (64) .... skills,	ADD
according to the (65) .... requirements of its new	PERSON
companion.	

Vocabulary Extension

A Vocabulary Building

Complete the unfinished words in the following sentences. All the words and phrases are related to services.

1 I can't accept a ch........................ because I don't have my own bank acc........................ .
2 Henry lives off the int........................ on the money he has deposited in the bank.
3 The couple made a with........................ from their bank and disappeared.
4 My application for a bank l........................ to buy a new car was turned down, but I was able to get a mort........................ to buy a house.
5 As I couldn't attend the wedding I sent a tel........................ to congratulate the bride and groom.
6 I'd send the document by reg........................ letter if I were you.
7 My phone's been dis........................ because I couldn't pay the b........................, I have also reached the limit on my cr........................ card.
8 If someone from the electricity board calls to read the me........................, ask for proof of identification.
9 There was a po........................ cut during last night's storm.
10 The water level in the reser........................ dropped during the heatwave and the town's water sup........................ was dangerously low.

B Word Use

Use the words on the left to complete the sentences on the right. Make sure the word is in the correct form.

1 **sole** / **single** / **unique**

a He is asked whether he's married or .... almost every .... day.
b The .... survivor was a three-month-old baby.
c This is a .... opportunity for you to learn Japanese.

2 **estimate** / **measurement** / **calculation** / **judgement**

a They fear their boss so much that they daren't question his ....
b I can't possibly do these .... in my head.
c The builder's original .... for roof repairs was £1,500.
d Check to see whether these .... for the new carpet are correct.

3 **recall** / **memorise** / **remind**

a That's odd! I don't .... meeting him at your party.
b Would you .... me to call my agent, please?
c It was easy to .... the number as it was my date of birth!

4 **cause** / **reason** / **purpose**

a What was the .... of his visit?
b Nobody knows what the .... of the fire was.
c He didn't tell me the .... for his absence.

5 **surely** / **likely** / **possible** / **certainly**

a She's not .... to be at home until six.
b .... you're not going to eat that, are you?
c It's .... not a new idea, but it's a good one.
d Is it .... to travel at the speed of light?

C Use of Prepositions

as *at* *from* *in (x 2)* *of (x 2)* *with*

1 If you're not familiar .... the procedure, I'll help you.
2 It's the same .... the one I bought.
3 They were aware .... the risks when they invested in the company.
4 I just can't prevent water .... getting in when it rains heavily.
5 We're expecting an increase .... the number of tourists coming to our hotel this year.
6 I'm not very fond .... shrimps, but I know Wendy is.
7 How can you expect Peter to take part .... the race with a pulled muscle?
8 You'll get the report by Friday .... the latest.

D Word Formation

I Use the word in capitals at the end of each sentence to form a word that fits in the space in the sentence.

1	There are no .... reasons why we shouldn't leave early.	ADD
2	.... of the project is likely to be delayed due to a lack of funds.	COMPLETE
3	He wants his .... but he also wants to rely on his parents at times.	DEPEND
4	Don't criticise him because he'll take it	PERSON
5	Are you going to football .... tonight?	TRAIN

II Choose the odd word out from the following groups of words according to how they form nouns.

1	educate	accept	participate	translate
2	amuse	embarrass	adjust	conserve
3	able	familiar	brave	similar
4	decide	revise	minor	divide
5	survive	explode	betray	remove
6	proceed	behave	fail	sign

Hints on note-taking/blank-filling (Part 2)

You must complete notes with gaps in them, incomplete statements, or questions. You do not need to write a full sentence or answer because three words is normally the maximum necessary.

Approach
You are given time to read through the question. Try and guess what sort of information has to go in each gap. The size of the gap should be used as a guide to how many words need to be used. You should fill in the gaps the first time you listen. Do not hesitate. Fill in the gap as quickly as possible. The second time you listen should be used to check your answers, not fill in the gaps. Spelling must be correct when a name is spelt letter by letter.

Pre-exam preparation
Practise note-taking while listening. Develop your own system for noting down things very quickly. Most questions involve writing a word or phrase that you actually hear on the cassette. You are not expected to rephrase what you hear in your own words.

Remember
If one question causes you a problem, continue listening – other questions may not provide any difficulty. You can then pay special attention to the missing question on the second listening.

Part 1

You will hear people talking in eight different situations. For questions **1-8**, choose the best answer, **A**, **B** or **C**.

1 You hear part of a radio news item. What feature did the two robbers have in common?

A They both had curly hair.
B They both had a big nose.
C They both had a long chin.

[ ] 1

2 You hear a man asking for help in a supermarket. What is his problem?

A He can't read the label.
B He doesn't know whether the product is good.
C He doesn't know how much the product costs.

[ ] 2

3 You hear two people talking about a new car. What does the woman particularly like about it?

A It doesn't make much noise.
B It is fast.
C It has a lot of safety features.

[ ] 3

4 You hear two people discussing a painting in an art gallery. What does the woman say about it?

A The artist has produced better work.
B The artist painted it at a time of great stress.
C She would like to own it.

[ ] 4

5 You are listening to someone demonstrating a scientific principle to children at a science museum. What is she demonstrating?

A a helicopter
B a rocket
C a balloon

[ ] 5

6 You hear two people talking about a film while waiting in a queue. What does the woman think the film will be like?

A exciting
B amusing
C terrifying

[ ] 6

7 You hear a woman checking into a hotel. What can you say about her?

A She always stays in the Presidential Suite.
B She always has the same kind of flowers in her room.
C She is always greeted by George when she checks in.

[ ] 7

8 You hear a man complaining to a shop assistant. What is his problem?

A He can't find the guarantee.
B He has damaged the receipt.
C He can't have the watch repaired immediately.

[ ] 8

Part 2

You will hear two recipes on a radio show. For questions **9-18**, complete the recipes. You will need to write a word, short phrase or a number in each box.

Savoury dish

Recipe for [**9**]

Ingredients: 100g grated cheese, 50g [**10**] breadcrumbs
300ml milk, 2 eggs, salt and pepper, ½ teaspoon mustard

What to do: Put the cheese and breadcrumbs into a basin.
After the cheese and breadcrumbs have been [**11**] pour milk over them.
Leave to stand for one hour.
Add beaten eggs, salt and pepper to the mixture.
Stir in mustard.
Pour into a pie dish and bake at [**12**]
Leave (25-30 mins) until risen and top is [**13**]
Serve at once. Enough for [**14**] people.

Sweet dish

Recipe for Apple Snow

Ingredients: 700g apples, one lemon, 100g caster sugar, [**15**] eggs, 1/3 cup of water.

What to do: Peel, core and cut apples into [**16**]
Put apples, lemon juice and water in a saucepan.
Cook the apples gently.
When cold beat in sugar until the mixture is [**17**]
Beat egg whites until they are stiff.
Put into serving dishes and decorate with [**18**]

Part 3

You will hear five different people talking about where they live. For questions **19-23**, choose which of the people **A-F** is speaking. Use the letters only once. There is one extra letter which you do not need to use.

A This person believes the disadvantages of where he/she lives are unimportant.

B This person has made a lot of changes to his/her house.

C This person hasn't really been affected by change.

D This person is sociable.

E This person would like to live somewhere more peaceful.

F This person has very little contact with other people.

Speaker	Answer	Question
Speaker 1		19
Speaker 2		20
Speaker 3		21
Speaker 4		22
Speaker 5		23

Part 4

You will hear part of an interview with two former professional footballers, David Armour and Jim McCall. Answer questions **24-30** by writing **D** (for David Armour)
J (for Jim McCall)
or **B** (for both David and Jim) in the boxes provided.

24	Who was expected to score goals?	**24**
25	Who was very popular with the supporters?	**25**
26	Who played for Southampton?	**26**
27	Who never got an FA Cup winners' medal?	**27**
28	Who played for his country?	**28**
29	Who has never managed a football team?	**29**
30	Who believes football has grown into a business?	**30**

Hints on comparing pictures (Part 2)

In this part of the examination the student has the opportunity to have his/her individual long turn. You must talk on your own about two photographs for about one minute. You should not describe the photographs in detail, but you should comment on them and give some personal reaction to them. You must also comment briefly on your fellow candidate's photographs.

Approach
Talk methodically about the two photographs and make sure what you say follows on logically from your previous statement. Remember, a minute is not a long time so if the Interlocutor interrupts you while you are still talking, don't worry because you have probably done well!

Pre-exam preparation
Practise commenting on photographs you see in the newspapers or magazines you read, or the posters you see advertising products in the streets, etc.

Remember
If the photographs surprise you, show surprise – your voice should reflect your feelings and attitude.

Part 1 (About 3 minutes)

Ask and answer the following questions with a partner.

- Do you have a large family or a small family?
- Do you wish you had a larger family?
- Can you tell me something about your family?
- Do you see your uncles, aunts and cousins very often?
- Where is your family from?

Part 2 (About 4 minutes)

Practise speaking about the photographs. The photos for Test Two are on page 179.

Candidate A, here are your two photographs. They show different types of holiday. Please let Candidate B have a look at them. Candidate A, I'd like you to compare and contrast these photographs, saying what you think are the advantages of going on each of these holidays (approximately one minute).

Candidate B, could you please tell us which of these holidays you would prefer to go on (approximately 20 seconds).

Candidate B, here are your two photographs. They show different kinds of food. Please let Candidate A have a look at them. Candidate B, I'd like you to compare and contrast these two photographs, saying which is the better diet (approximately one minute).

Candidate A, could you please tell us which of these kinds of food you prefer (approximately twenty seconds).

Part 3 (About 3 minutes)

Discuss the following with a partner.

Imagine you have been asked by a relative who owns a hotel to suggest where in the hotel the pictures shown on the opposite page could be hung. Talk to each other about which picture(s) could be hung in the reception area, the dining room, the lounge and a typical room. It is not necessary to agree with each other.

Part 4 (About 4 minutes)

Give each other your opinions on the following questions.

- How important is art today?
- How important is it to know what the artist is trying to say?
- Should the history of art be taught at school?
- Can anyone learn how to paint or is it necessary to have natural talent?
- What kind of person makes a good artist?

Hints on working with a gapped text (Part 3)

In Part 3 of the reading paper you will read a text from which paragraphs or sentences have been removed. The missing paragraphs or sentences are provided in a jumbled order and you will decide from where in the text the paragraphs or sentences have been removed. This tests an understanding of how texts are structured.

Approach
Read the whole text first. Look for clues before and after the missing paragraph or sentence which link the text. Look for something that fits into the description, or for a logical sequence of ideas. Check for reference back to pronouns. Make sure that tenses fit logically. As you work through the task, you may find it difficult to find the answer to a particular question. This could mean that you have made a mistake with an earlier question. Therefore, be prepared to review your choices until you are really sure that the text 'flows' with all the correct answers. Read the part of the text with the paragraph or sentence you have chosen to fit in the gap and make sure it makes sense. Answer all the questions.

Pre-exam preparation
Practise this type of exercise by removing sentences from a text and asking a partner to find which sentence fits where. Make up sentences of your own that could fit! Pay careful attention as to how a text is structured while you are reading.

Remember
The more you read, the more you will become familiar with the rhythms of the language. Choose something you are interested in and read for your own pleasure!

Part 1

You are going to read a book review. Choose the most suitable heading from the list **A-I** for each part (**1-7**) of the review. There is one extra heading which you do not need to use. There is an example at the beginning (**0**).

A	Much more frightened than normal
B	Living with snakes
C	The fear remains
D	A terrible end
E	Facing up to fear
F	Exceedingly poisonous
G	Testing for speed
H	Thrilling stories
I	A close call

Fear Comes in Bite-size Pieces

If you are frightened of snakes, don't read this book.

Snakebite Survivors' Club
by Jeremy Seal
Picador, £16.99, 377 pp

0 I

Snake stories among old soldiers who served in Africa are two a penny. A relative of mine, for instance, was driving in Kenya when he decided to stop and stretch his legs. It was not until he was out of the car that he realised that a few feet away was a black-necked cobra, a nasty snake that spits venom at its victims' eyes, causing terrible pain and blindness. As he slowly backed away, the snake rose ready to strike. He got into the car and just as the window closed, the snake spat and a dose of venom hit the glass in front of my relative's eyes.

1

Jeremy Seal though is not interested in near-misses; *The Snakebite Survivors' Club* is about the real thing. Fear of snakes is universal but Seal's terror was debilitating; snakes haunted him and despite living in Gloucestershire he came to believe he was going to die of snakebite.

2

Torn between terror and fascination, he decided to confront his phobia by tracking down people who had been bitten by the most venomous snakes in the world and lived. This drastic therapy concentrated on four snakes in four continents: the American rattlesnake, the Indian cobra, the African black mamba and the Australian taipan.

3

Jeremy Seal writes beautifully. He is adept at scene setting and at building tension. As he crosses the earth, his narrative mixes travel, history, snake fact, fiction and thriller. The body count rises as people become victims of serpents.

4

Given the toxicity of Seal's chosen snakes it is little wonder that the survivors he meets were in some way remarkable. The taipan, for example, can deliver enough venom in one bite to kill 12,000 guinea pigs; on a human this results in paralysis and death from heart failure.

5

Running throughout his book is the story of Darlene Summerford Collins, whose husband decided to kill her by forcing her to put her hand repeatedly into a cage of rattlesnakes. Her horrific ordeal, described in detail, acts like the music in *Jaws*.

6

Among all the stories are scenes of farce. In 1906, a naturalist decided to find out just how fast a mamba could move. He told his assistant to get ready to run while he threw earth at the snake. Enraged, the snake pursued the assistant while the naturalist timed the chase. The experiment had to be cut short when the man fell and the snake was shot as it was about to strike. The mamba had reached eleven kph.

7

This book may have helped Jeremy Seal to come to terms with his own fear, but he has done nothing for mine. I won't be going to America, India, Africa, or Australia in the foreseeable future.

Part 2

You are going to read an article about cooking. For questions **8-14**, choose the answer **A**, **B**, **C** or **D** which you think fits best according to the text.

It Can be Cool in the Kitchen

During my adolescence I was fascinated by food, but my curiosity had more to do with greed than a desire to cook. The only hint of my future in the world of cooking came on Wednesday afternoons in our school in our domestic science lessons.

These days it seems the subject is becoming a thing of the past, but when I was at school it was compulsory and took place in the domestic science labs. There, hunger-crazed teenagers were taken through the procedures of old-fashioned baking, from rock buns to Victoria sponge and shortbread. I remember the smells – sweet, yeasty, buttery, baking smells – and the greed that propelled fingers around bowls of raw cake mixture, the final creations never quite the shape or size they should have been.

I excelled, if not in talent, then certainly in the greed department. Being aware of the fact that all food, burnt or otherwise, was duly taken back to the dormitory to be shared, I formed a plan. One week it consisted of emptying some green food colouring over my Madeira cake. The next it was inky-blue meringues. The other girls refused my offerings and I, for once, did not go to bed hungry.

Hunger is the greatest motive for the inexperienced cook. But many people are now worried that we are producing a generation without the slightest idea of how to cook – a generation that is frightened to cook. I have just received a leaflet from *Focus on Food*, which is running a campaign to get children back into the kitchen. Has television cooking become a substitute for the real thing? Is this an age where celebrity chefs have turned cooking into a sort of spectator sport, with dishes far too complicated for the beginner to copy?

I decided to ask my eldest daughter, Miranda, for her opinion. Do they feel strongly about the disappearing domestic science lesson? Are children learning enough about the importance of good cooking? Sociology and other 'new' subjects are all very well, but without the ability to cook, or to understand the pleasure and principles of good food and its relationship to good health, are we really preparing them for adult life?

Miranda started her cooking at the age of nine, when she decided to enter the Sainsbury's *Future Cook* competition. She was motivated by a different kind of greed: the first prize trip to Disney World.

The drawback, from the parental point of view, was that if she made it through to the regional finals, she would have to cook her meal in front of a panel of judges. Some 30,000 children entered and she made it through as the youngest regional finalist. Now she had to learn to cook. Her hands were not even big enough to grip the Sabatier and slice the onions. Six Saturdays running we ate the same lunch – mozzarella meatballs in fresh tomato sauce and blueberry and cinnamon custards.

First, she cooked by my side, then alone with timings and instructions. Finally, she went solo against the clock. The kitchen looked like Armageddon, but she had cracked it. The tiny becapped, aproned figure subsequently stood in an unknown Bristol hotel, looking like a professional who had been at the stove for years. She did not win, but she came home with £50 and the most valuable ingredient of them all: confidence.

8 What does the writer say about domestic science?

A Fewer schools teach it nowadays.
B It is compulsory in nearly all schools.
C It is normally taught on Wednesdays.
D Only traditional cooking is taught.

9 How did the students' cakes normally turn out?

A They were undercooked.
B They didn't smell right.
C They were too sweet.
D They didn't look right.

10 Why didn't the writer have to share her food with other students?

A They were on diets.
B She hid it from them.
C It didn't taste very nice.
D It looked unattractive.

11 What is *Focus on Food* currently trying to do?

A to get people to train as celebrity chefs
B to get people interested in television cooking
C to get people to cook from an early age
D to advertise for hotel chefs

12 Why does the writer think cooking is so important?

A It can save money.
B It helps develop relationships.
C It is a necessary part of life.
D It will produce more celebrity chefs.

13 Why did the writer's family have the same lunch six Saturdays running?

A It allowed Miranda to practise her cooking.
B It was the family's favourite meal.
C It was the only thing the family could cook.
D There was nothing else available.

14 What did Miranda gain from the competition?

A A prize for being the youngest winner.
B She was no longer afraid to cook.
C A chance to take a course in cooking for only £50.
D A certificate and a medal.

Part 3

You are going to read an article about exchanging items in shops. Eight sentences have been removed from the article. Choose from the sentences **A-I** the one which fits each gap (**15-21**). There is one extra sentence which you do not need to use. There is an example at the beginning (**0**).

When the Pyjamas don't Fit

Know your legal position before returning goods to the shops

We all regard receiving presents as a pleasant experience and yet it can be one of the most awkward. **0** I

All you can do is exchange it after your friend or relative has gone home. **15** ____ Worse still, the agreement on a sale is between the person who bought it and the shop.

16 ____ But an exchange is not always that simple because there has to be a good reason for it. Either the item has to be faulty or unsuitable for the job it was intended to do.

17 ____ You would have the right to return it and get your money back.

But if you are returning something, no matter what the reason, you will be expected to have proof of purchase. **18** ____ If all of these have been mislaid, you may have to rely on a witness.

Many big stores have a much more tolerant policy towards returns and see it as a gesture of goodwill to exchange items without question. Stores including *Marks & Spencer* and *HMV* are well know for their 'no argument' policy on returned goods. **19** ____

So if a shop or store refuses to exchange an item, to offer a refund or to give you a credit note, the retailer is likely to be within his legal rights unless there is something wrong with the item. **20** ____ You have every right to demand a cash refund or a replacement, but only if you have returned it within a 'reasonable' time.

Unfortunately, the law does not define what is meant by 'reasonable'. **21** ____ In any case if you return an item after what is considered a 'reasonable' time, then all you are legally entitled to is the cost of repair.

A Unfortunately, you have no right to change an item purchased just because it does not fit or is not to your liking.

B In that case, the boot is on the other foot.

C Some shops and stores expect things to be returned within a week of purchase, or at least a week from when you received them, while others may impose a much longer time limit.

D If the receipt cannot be found, then it is possible to use another proof of purchase such as a credit or debit card receipt.

E Without proof of purchase the shop would be within its rights to refuse to exchange it.

F So you will have to tell your favourite aunt that the pyjamas do not fit or the pullover is a colour you would never wear.

G However, shoppers should remember this is a privilege, not a right.

H For example, if the buyer was told that a food mixer was capable of kneading bread and later found out it was not, then action could be taken.

I It is often difficult to look pleased when you receive a gift which is entirely useless, the wrong size or unlike anything you would buy for yourself.

Part 4

You are going to read an article about five lottery or pools winners. For questions **22-35**, choose from the people (**A-I**). The people may be chosen more than once. When more than one answer is required, these may be given in any order. There is an example at the beginning (**0**).

Which of the winners

celebrated his win at home?	**0** A	
kept his win a secret?	**22**	
performed an act of generosity immediately?	**23**	**24**
had a bitter experience after his win?	**25**	
was able to keep his win a secret?	**26**	
spent all the money very quickly?	**27**	
is unlikely to play the lottery now?	**28**	
was abroad when he received news of his win?	**29**	
followed professional advice after his win?	**30**	**31**
is unlikely to make the same mistake as he made before his win?	**32**	
received a great deal of publicity after his win?	**33**	**34**
has been contacted by people he didn't know before his win?	**35**	

Hitting the Jackpot

Five previous winners talk about winning the lottery and pools

A Barry, 46

I was working in Germany when I found out about the win. We were working on a building site and it was Friday evening. A few mates had come into my room and we were having a laugh. It was freezing. We had no heating. Then I got a telegram from my wife saying we'd won £5 million in the lottery. My mates thought it was a joke, but my wife doesn't kid around when money is involved. I said they could take my pay packet and split the money among themselves and I left for England. My wife and children waited for me before they celebrated. Things are a lot different now, I can tell you!

B Peter, 24

I'd got out of prison about six weeks before I won. I got over £10m. I was in for stealing cars, joy-riding, so I bought myself four new cars, including a Ferrari and a Ford Cosworth. I got my brother a Jag straight away – he'd always wanted one. Then I bought a big house and a helicopter. It's in the back garden now. Since I won I have had several proposals of marriage from all over the country and I don't think they want me for my brains!

C Jack, 62

At the time, in 1962, that is, it was news. I won £250,000 on the pools. It seems like chicken feed now, but it was a lot then. It was in all the newspapers. I went through the winnings in less than three years and ended up broke. Those three years were great. I still haven't changed my mind. If it happened again, I'd do the same. I don't regret what I did even though many people think I'm mad. I had the time of my life, so did some of my close friends – and they're still my friends to this day.

D Nigel, 65

I got eight draws on the pools back in 1984. We hit the jackpot – £758,000. I thought I was dreaming at first. I checked and double-checked. We'd filled in the no publicity box – we didn't want to announce it. Anyway, a man from the pools called on us on Monday morning and advised us what to do with the money. We invested it as he suggested and now we don't have any financial worries. Neither my friends nor my family found out so there was no problem. Not even my children know. They'll just get a shock when they read my will!

E Mushtaq, 47

It was a record win at the time of £17 million. We tried to keep it a secret, but the news was leaked. What happened next is common knowledge. My wife and I separated and there was a court case to decide who should have the money. A lot of it went to our lawyers; we each had an army of them. It was unpleasant to say the least. I've tried to get on with my life but it's not been easy. Perhaps it will be forgotten one day. One thing is for sure, though, I don't want to go through the same thing again!

Hints on writing an article

Articles are usually written for magazines or newsletters. They will probably be written for someone who is interested in the same things as you. You should aim to interest the reader and include some opinions.

Approach
Read the question carefully. In this test you are asked to state a preference and to give reasons for your choice. Your first paragraph might state what you believe to be the general feeling for holidays (for example 'Many people prefer to go abroad for their holidays ...') followed by your own personal preference ('On the other hand, I like to stay in my own country and explore areas that are off the beaten track.'). Then think about more detailed reasons why you made your choice. This is your chance to show the examiner the range of vocabulary and expressions you know in the language. Don't forget to add a short concluding paragraph to your article.

Pre-examination preparation
In order to write a good article, you should already have read several different types of article in English magazines. Each time you read an article, look out for expressions, vocabulary items and ways of linking that make the reading interesting. Look at the content of the paragraphs and see how the writer has approached the subject. You will soon find your own writing improving if you adopt some of those techniques.

Remember
Part of the marks you get for the writing task are related to the effect your composition has on the target reader. If material is not appropriate, or you do not answer the question properly, it will be difficult for the examiner to give you higher marks.

Part 1

You **must** answer this question.

1 You are on a committee that organises social events at an international student college. The college allows the students to organise one excursion of their choice every year. Read the note from the secretary of the committee, Joanne, and the college regulations concerning excursions. Then write to the Principal, asking for permission to go on the excursion and giving him some information about the excursion.

Sorry you weren't at Monday's meeting. We decided to go to Chester for the day – I hope you approve of our decision. You'll have to be careful when you write to Mr Walker because there were a few unpleasant incidents (drinking on the way back) during last year's trip to York. By the way, we've chosen a date to coincide with the races!! (On second thoughts, it'll probably be best if you don't mention that.) Anyway, here are the decisions we've made:

Date:	16th April
Depart:	8.30 am
Return:	10 pm
Destination:	Chester
Visits:	Zoo, historical sites, castle, shops
No of Students:	66 (one coach enough)
Staff:	Mr and Mrs Braithwaite

Thank you.

Jo

COLLEGE REGULATIONS – Excursions

One excursion per year may be arranged by students provided that:

- full details are submitted to the Principal at least one calendar month before the date of the excursion
- students are accompanied by two members of staff per coach
- no alcohol is consumed on the coach

Write a **letter** of between **120** and **180** words in an appropriate style. Do not write any addresses.

Part 2

Write an answer to **one** of the questions **2-5** in this part. Write your answer in **120-180** words in an appropriate style.

2 You have seen this announcement in an international student magazine.

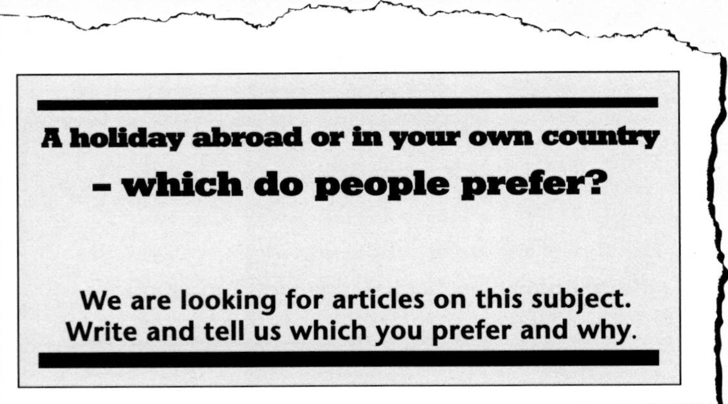
A holiday abroad or in your own country
– which do people prefer?

We are looking for articles on this subject.
Write and tell us which you prefer and why.

Write your **article**.

3 You have decided to enter a short story competition. The competition rules say that the story must begin with the following words:

"I'm afraid I can't start the car," said Chris.

Write your **story** for the competition.

4 You are going to visit your English pen friend but you have had to make some changes to your original plans. Write a letter to your pen friend, telling him or her about the changes and the reasons for them. You should also ask your pen friend how these changes will affect what you were planning to do together.

Write your **letter**.

5 Background reading texts

Answer **one** of the following two questions based on your reading of **one** of the set books. Your answer should contain enough detail to make it clear to someone who may not have read the book.

Either (a) Your college is going to put on a play based on the book you have read and your teacher has asked for some suggestions and advice. Write a composition, giving your opinion about which scene would be the most suitable and which would be the least suitable for a theatrical production.

or (b) Surprises make a book interesting. Write a composition describing a part of the book which turned out differently from what you expected and stating what you thought would happen and why.

Hints on 'key' word transformations

You must fill in a gap with between two and five words to complete a sentence which means the same as a prompt sentence. One of the words used to fill the gap must be the 'key' word given. The 'key' word must not be changed in any way. This tests several items such as passive voice, conditionals, modals, phrasal verbs and lexical phrases. For example:

It wasn't easy for Karen to complete the course.
difficulty

Karen .... the course.

The gap can be filled by 'had difficulty in completing' and not 'found it difficult to complete' because the 'key' word cannot be changed.

Approach
Read the prompt sentence carefully to understand exactly what it means. Look at the 'key' word and decide how it can be used in connection with the prompt sentence. Finally, make sure the phrase you have found fits between the beginning and end of the sentence to be completed. Remember to check your spelling.

Pre-exam preparation
Develop an awareness of synonymous expressions by rephrasing what you read and practising this type of exercise. When you have finished all the 'key' word transformations in this book, you could go back to the first test and see if you can 'transform' your answer back to the original sentence!

Remember
Contractions, like 'don't, can't, won't' etc, are counted as TWO words. Don't forget, however, that 'cannot' is one word.

Part 1

For questions **1-15**, read the text below and decide which answer **A**, **B**, **C** or **D** best fits each space. There is an example at the beginning (**0**).

Example:

0	**A** before	**B** since	**C** ago	**D** sooner

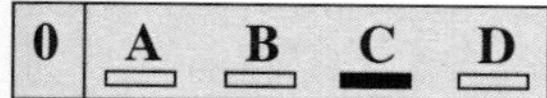

Off to an Island

Several years (0) .... while I was visiting Athens for a few weeks, I decided to spend a whole day on a (1) .... island. The weather (2) .... had predicted that it would be a scorching hot day so I (3) .... off early in the morning.

Even though I arrived at the port in plenty of time, I was forced to sit on the top (4) .... because other passengers who had (5) .... to the boat earlier filled the lower ones. Soon after the boat had departed, somebody came round with raffle tickets. There were, as far as I could make (6) ...., two prizes: a bag of fresh fish and several (7) .... of chocolate. I bought a ticket, not (8) .... to win as I had never won anything in a raffle (9) ....

Some time later the person who had sold the tickets (10) .... the winning numbers. To my great surprise, I had won the chocolate. I was naturally delighted, but (11) .... how I could prevent it from (12) .... in the intense heat. Realising that I could not possible eat it all myself, I (13) .... it with the passengers sitting near me. In return, they offered me sandwiches and (14) .... drinks.

(15) ...., it was a pleasant start to a memorable day with my new acquaintances.

1	**A**	nearby	**B**	close	**C**	neighbourly	**D**	joining
2	**A**	prediction	**B**	prophecy	**C**	forecast	**D**	foresight
3	**A**	went	**B**	left	**C**	departed	**D**	set
4	**A**	deck	**B**	layer	**C**	floor	**D**	storey
5	**A**	reached	**B**	arrived	**C**	approached	**D**	got
6	**A**	up	**B**	out	**C**	for	**D**	over
7	**A**	bars	**B**	slices	**C**	cartons	**D**	packets
8	**A**	thinking	**B**	expecting	**C**	waiting	**D**	anticipating
9	**A**	again	**B**	before	**C**	since	**D**	already
10	**A**	stated	**B**	remarked	**C**	told	**D**	announced
11	**A**	thought	**B**	questioned	**C**	wondered	**D**	regarded
12	**A**	dissolving	**B**	liquefying	**C**	melting	**D**	spreading
13	**A**	separated	**B**	divided	**C**	distributed	**D**	shared
14	**A**	soft	**B**	light	**C**	bubbly	**D**	sparkling
15	**A**	In conclusion	**B**	In contrast	**C**	All in all	**D**	In addition

Part 2

For questions **16-30**, read the text below and think of the word which best fits each space. Use only one word in each space. There is an example at the beginning (**0**).

Emperor Penguins

At about 1.20 metres (0) ....tall...... and weighing about thirty kilos, the Emperor penguin is (16) .... largest of seventeen penguin species. It is also the only animal (17) .... from the Weddel seal which is (18) .... to survive the hostile Antarctic weather all year round. In order to survive at temperatures which (19) .... fall to -40 °C, the Emperor penguin lives in large colonies in which the birds keep from freezing to death by sticking close to (20) .... other. These penguins live on fish in the Weddel Sea and are capable (21) .... diving to depths of 500 metres to hunt.

The female lays one egg, about the same (22) .... as a tennis ball, in March. Then she goes off to feed for two months, leaving the male to look (23) .... the egg. (24) .... is no nest. The male balances the egg on his feet, (25) .... densely feathered flesh keeps the cold out. In this period (26) .... is possible for the male to lose up to half its body weight. The females return just as the chicks start demanding food when it is their turn to (27) .... care of the small bird. The young bird spends the first two months in the warmth of a pouch – rather (28) .... a baby kangaroo.

About half the chicks survive and (29) .... they reach adulthood, they can live for (30) .... than twenty years.

Part 3

For questions **31-40**, complete the second sentence so that it has a similar meaning to the first sentence, using the word given. **Do not change the word given**. You must use between two and five words including the word given. There is an example at the beginning (**0**).

0 I've never been asked that question before.
person

You're .... who has asked me that question.

The gap can be filled by the words 'the first person who has' so you write:

0	*the first person*

31 I want you to keep it secret.
rather

I .... tell anyone about it.

32 The team is going to postpone the match until next Saturday.
put

The match .... off until next Monday.

33 "Renting a cottage would be a solution to your problems, Jasmine," said Anne.
suggested

Anne .... a cottage.

34 My new teacher was older than I had expected.
as

My new teacher .... I had expected.

35 The travel company includes a visit to Hyde Park in its tour of London.
is

A visit to Hyde Park .... the travel company's tour of London.

36 I haven't seen Barry since the party.
time

The last .... at the party.

37 Some men and women were waiting in the queue.
few

There .... waiting in the queue.

38 It's possible that she didn't remember how to use the computer.
might

She .... how to use the computer.

39 We found it easy to make friends with the locals.
difficulty

We .... friends with the locals.

40 Hilary's parents did everything to help her when she moved house.
had

Hilary .... when she moved house.

Part 4

For questions **41-55**, read the text below and look carefully at each line. Some of the lines are correct and some have a word which should not be there. If a line is correct put a tick (✓) by the number. If a line has a word which should not be there, write the word. There are two examples at the beginning (**0** and **00**).

A FOOLISH PRACTICE

0 There are few things that annoy me more than seeing three,
00 or even four people (usually two parents and a child or two of
41 children) riding on a motorcycle or scooter without helmets.
42 Whenever I see this, I really feel like stopping to ask about the
43 motorcyclist if he or she has thought about the dangers of what
44 they are doing. Although I am tempted to not do this, I have
45 never done so. I just wonder why do they do it. My friends
46 say that these people believe that they drive so carefully that
47 there is not much chance of them being involved in an accident.
48 This, of course, is not logical reason because many accidents involving
49 motorcycles or scooters are not being the fault of the motorcyclist.
50 Many drivers do not see motorcycles until the last moment and
51 when they do, they are panic. This often causes an accident,
52 the result of which is much more serious for the person or people
53 on the two-wheeler than that it is for the car driver. If this
54 has happened to a motorcyclist with his family, it could result
55 in a fatal accident. In my opinion, the only one way to stop this
foolishness is to introduce new laws and enforce them.

0	✓
00	of
41	
42	
43	
44	
45	
46	
47	
48	
49	
50	
51	
52	
53	
54	
55	

Part 5

For questions **56-65**, read the text below. Use the word given in capitals at the end of each line to form a word that fits in the space in the same line. There is an example at the beginning (**0**).

The Memory Stealers

Up to now, the (0) ......*difficulties*....... in a fisherman's working life have been	DIFFICULT
quite obvious, but now they face a new threat from (56)	MICROSCOPE
plant-like organisms. These creatures, which are (57) .... to the	VISION
naked eye have been (58) .... as causing American fishermen to	IDENTIFY
'lose their memory'. (59) .... investigating the phenomenon	SCIENCE
observed that the fishermen affected became so (60) .... that	FORGET
their lives were thrown into (61) .... Amongst other things, they	CONFUSE
were unable to remember to take important fishing (62) .... with	EQUIP
them when they left for work and they (63) .... forgot where they	FREQUENCY
were going in the middle of a journey. (64) .... the memory loss is	LUCK
reversible. Within six months the fishermen's (65) .... had	BEHAVE
returned to normal.	

Vocabulary Extension

A Vocabulary Building

Complete the unfinished words in the following sentences. All the words are related to food.

1 Frank is so gr.................. that even three port.................. of chips aren't enough for him.
2 I prefer bo.................. or ro.................. potatoes to chips.
3 Don't gu.................. your drink, s.................. it.
4 It's difficult for me to dig.................. sp.................. dishes so I often end up with a stomach ache after eating them.
5 Sandra's a veg.................. but she still eats j.................. food from time to time.
6 I'd like my steak ra.................. , Carol would like hers w.................. d.................. and Pam would rather have lamb ch.................. .
7 If the lemon drink is too bi.................. , then add a little sugar to sw.................. it.
8 I had a prawn cocktail for a st.................. , gri.................. fish for a main c.................. and ice cream for des.................. .
9 The rec.................. you gave me can't be correct because some ingr.................. are missing.
10 The dish was so ta.................. that I asked for a second he.................. .

B Word Use

Use the words on the left to complete the sentences on the right. Make sure the word is in the correct form.

1 **deck** **layer** **floor** **storey**

a The cake looked wonderful with a thick .... of cream on top.
b I hope the lift isn't out of order because she lives on the twentieth ....
c Most people in the area live in a two- .... house.
d Why don't you get out of your cabin and get some fresh air on ....

2 **bar** **slice** **carton** **packet**

a I'd rather have a piece of fruit than a .... of chocolate.
b Could you get an extra .... of milk for me, please?
c Did you remember to put a .... of biscuits in the picnic basket?
d My mother used to put two .... of ham in my sandwiches.

3 **dissolve** **liquefy** **melt** **spread**

a The ice wouldn't have .... if you'd put it back in the freezer.
b Don't .... the jam so thickly on your sandwich.
c Sugar will not .... in petrol.
d Gases can be .... at very low temperatures or very high pressures.

4 **separate** **divide** **distribute** **share**

a This piece of land will be .... into four plots, one for each of you.
b If we win, we'll .... the money.
c He spent last summer .... leaflets for a large supermarket.
d In this part of the factory we .... gold from other metals.

5 **soft** **light** **sparkling**

a You should stick to .... drinks if you are driving.
b Drinks can be described as .... if they are low in calories or alcohol content.
c .... wine sells quite well in Britain.

C Use of Prepositions

Use the prepositions below to complete the sentences which follow.

at *in* *of (x 2)* *on (x 2)* *to* *with*

1 Once we've agreed .... a price, the deal can go through.
2 Whales are capable .... communicating with each other over long distances.
3 Laura's pretty keen .... art so I expect she'll want to visit the gallery.
4 I'm sure your mother wouldn't approve .... your behaviour.
5 Fox hunting is an activity which is normally associated .... the rich.
6 My sister learned to swim .... the age of four.
7 Nigel's just not interested .... tennis.
8 Borrowing money continuously is not a solution .... your problems.

D Word Formation

I Use the word in capitals at the end of each sentence to form a word that fits in the space in the sentence.

1 The robbers managed to escape in all the .... CONFUSE
2 Andrew's so .... that he always buys birthday presents a day late. FORGET
3 Just because it's .... it doesn't mean it doesn't exist. VISION
4 They were very proud of .... after winning the tournament. SELF
5 Without the right .... you can't hope to take good photos. EQUIP

II Choose the odd word out from the following groups of words according to how they form adjectives.

1	microscope	atmosphere	base	psychology
2	suit	rely	misery	compete
3	poison	profit	disaster	fury
4	value	profession	nature	politics
5	peace	prefer	skill	plenty
6	attract	disgust	argument	destroy

Hints on multiple matching (Part 3)

You will hear five extracts of about half a minute (either monologues or interacting speakers). All the extracts will have one theme in common. Your task will be to match options from a list to each of the extracts.

Approach
Read through the options carefully and underline any key words. Really try to understand what each speaker is saying. Attempt to make your choice on the first listening. When the recording is repeated, you should check that you have got the correct answers. Similar details are likely to be mentioned in each of the extracts – these are designed to distract you, so listen very carefully.

Pre-exam preparation
Listen to as much spoken English as you can. Television and radio can help, but don't forget that many people speak English around you every day, so try listening in (discreetly!) to conversations going on around you on the bus, on the beach, in cafés, etc.

Remember
If you discover that you've made a wrong choice for one of the questions, don't forget that this could possibly have an effect on your other answers. So, check your answers carefully, especially on the second listening.

Part 1

You will hear people talking in eight different situations. For questions **1-8**, choose the best answer, **A**, **B** or **C**.

1 You hear a conversation between two friends. Why couldn't the woman contact her ex-colleague?

A She made a mistake when she wrote down the telephone number.
B The number she had no longer existed.
C Someone else was living in his old house.

1

2 You hear an announcement at a railway station. What does the announcer say?

A Passengers for Bristol Temple Meads will be leaving earlier than expected.
B Passengers travelling further than Exeter should go to platform 7.
C Passengers travelling to Exeter should stay where they are.

2

3 You hear a man reporting a lost wallet. What does he say?

A The last time he saw it was when he was on the train.
B He thinks it was in the jacket he left on the train.
C He believes someone stole it.

3

4 You hear two people talking about saving money. How does the woman manage to save?

A She plans her spending carefully.
B She earns more money than the man.
C She thinks it is essential to save.

4

5 It's half-time in a football match when you hear two people talking. What does the man think the final result will be ?

A His team will win.
B The match will end in a draw.
C His team will lose.

5

6 You hear two people talking about a car show. What complaint did the woman have?

A It was overcrowded.
B It was too expensive.
C It was too big.

6

7 You hear a man talking about his job. What is his job?

A a security guard
B a traffic warden
C a plain clothes policeman

7

8 You hear a man talking about a sport he used to practise. What sport was it?

A tennis
B golf
C basketball

8

Part 2

You will hear part of a geography lecture. For questions **9-18**, complete the sentences. You will need to write a word, short phrase or number in each box.

NEWFOUNDLAND (LABRADOR)

The first Europeans arrived after being sent off course by [**9**]

Reports of rich fish stocks brought fishing fleets in the [**10**] century.

Until 1763 there was a struggle for power between [**11**]

Traded goods in the area included [**12**]

Places like Raman and Hebron have become [**13**]

Labrador is approximately the same size as [**14**]

The area depends on the production of [**15**]

Unemployment in some towns has reached [**16**]

Most people in the region travel by [**17**]

The region is trying to attract tourists who like [**18**]

Part 3

You will hear five different people talking about their leisure activities. For questions **19-23**, choose which of the people **A-F** is speaking. Use the letters only once. There is one extra letter which you do not need to use.

A This person's hobby is very expensive.

B This person believes his/her pastime is more than just a hobby.

C This person is considered strange because of his/her hobby.

D This person didn't expect his/her hobby to be so exciting.

E This person took up his/her hobby at a young age.

F This person has earned some money from his/her hobby.

Speaker 1		19
Speaker 2		20
Speaker 3		21
Speaker 4		22
Speaker 5		23

Part 4

You will hear three people planning their summer holiday. Answer questions **24-30** by writing

J (for Jennie)
M (for Michael) or
H (for Harry) in the boxes provided.

24 Who makes a complaint? [ ] **24**

25 Who makes a suggestion which has nothing to do with holidays? [ ] **25**

26 Who confirms what someone else said? [ ] **26**

27 Who doesn't agree with someone else's suggestion? [ ] **27**

28 Who becomes quite aggressive and sarcastic? [ ] **28**

29 Who apologises more than once? [ ] **29**

30 Who makes the same suggestion twice? [ ] **30**

Hints on speaking with a partner using a visual prompt (Part 3)

This is a collaborative activity where you must talk to your fellow candidate in order to complete a task set by the interlocutor. The task may involve planning, problem solving, decision making, speculating, etc. You will be given photographs, diagrams, plans or line drawings to use during the conversation.

Approach
The main point here is to work towards the completion of the task with your partner. Express your opinions and attitudes clearly to your partner in order to promote discussion. Remember, use your personality to good effect and don't be frightened to ask questions. Get involved with the task and forget the examiner. Don't be surprised if he/she interrupts you when your time is up! You will get more marks if you take a full and active part in the interaction. You are also expected to develop your partner's comments (which means you will have to LISTEN carefully). You should also invite your partner to respond.

Preparation
Practise this kind of task in class as much as possible. Your teacher should ensure that you get plenty of practice working in groups before the exam. It's not always easy to speak in a foreign language to someone else who speaks your own language, but you really need to practice this as you will not be given any other choice in the exam.

Part 1 (About 3 minutes)

Ask and answer the following questions with a partner.

- Can you tell me something about yourself?
- What do you enjoy most about your studies?
- How much time do you study?
- Which subjects do you find most difficult?
- What qualifications will you need for the job you hope to do?

Part 2 (About 4 minutes)

Practise speaking about the photographs that you will find on page 180.

Candidate A, here are your two photographs. They show people doing different jobs. Please let Candidate B have a look at them. Candidate A, I'd like you to compare and contrast these photographs, saying what you think about these jobs (approximately one minute).

Candidate B, could you please tell us which job you would prefer to do (approximately twenty seconds).

Candidate B, here are your two photographs. They show children at special celebrations. Please let Candidate A have a look at them. Candidate B, I'd like you to compare and contrast these two photographs saying what you think these children's feelings are (approximately one minute).

Candidate A, could you please tell us which celebration would make you feel happier (approximately twenty seconds).

Part 3 (About 3 minutes)

Discuss the following with a partner.

Imagine that a youth club – a place where young people can spend their free time – is going to be built in your area. Talk to each other about which of the pastimes shown on the opposite page would be the most popular and which would be the least popular. It is not necessary to agree with each other.

Part 4 (About 4 minutes)

Give each other your opinions about the following questions.

- How can watching television be harmful?
- In what way can reading be a good pastime?
- Is it better to watch an event on television or see it live?
- How important is it to make good use of your free time?
- How are pastimes today different from what they used to be?

Hints on multiple matching (Part 4)

You must answer each question by referring to the part of a text in which the answer appears. This tests your ability to locate specific information in a text.

Approach
Scan through the text first to get an idea of what each part contains. Then look at the questions and scan again for the answers in the text. Don't try reading every word of the text – you won't have time and it is completely unnecessary. However, you may find similar information in different parts of the text, so you should check carefully to make sure that your choice matches the question you are being asked. You may find that you remember where some of the answers are. Others may be more difficult to locate. Remember, the question may not contain exactly the same vocabulary as the text. For example, the text may read 'I think it is better to go abroad' and the question might be 'Who believes there is an advantage to leaving for another country?' Always justify your answer and answer all the questions.

Pre-exam preparation
Practise reading texts and stating exactly where in the text a particular reference is made or opinion is given.

Remember
Pay attention to the complete meaning of the statements or questions in Part 4.

Part 1

You are going to read a newspaper article about a spaceship. Choose the most suitable heading from the list **A-I** for each part (**1-7**) of the article. There is one extra heading which you do not need to use. There is an example at the beginning (**0**).

A	Checking the water
B	Qualified tasters only
C	The best in every way
D	A set routine
E	Ready for action
F	Returning a verdict
G	Satisfying the requirements
H	In complete agreement
I	You must be joking!

Château Thames

Max Davies meets the water tasters

0 I

When I was told that there were people who tasted water for a living, I thought someone was pulling my leg. Water is water. It must be the most boring drink in the world.

1

Not that they share that view at Thames Water. The biggest water company in the country is naturally going to take pride in its product. What surprised me was how seriously they took the business of tasting. They are not just committed to producing the purest water possible, using the most up-to-date technology. They want it to taste good. They want to give their customers an aesthetically pleasing experience.

2

By the time I arrived in Reading at 10.30, the Fab Four of water tasting – Marilyn, Alison, Carol and Steve – had already assembled in a room marked 'Sensory Analysis'. They were wearing white lab coats and looked appropriately serious.

3

'We have had nothing to eat or drink since breakfast,' Alison told me. 'It would affect the validity of the tasting.' They meet like this every working day. When one is indisposed, a substitute is found. But it cannot be just anybody. Staff must have proven tasting ability before they are allowed, as it were, to pass water.

4

In front of the tasters, in unmarked phials, was the water they were going to sample. The samples had been selected at random. All the water that comes out of our taps goes through this process. It was one of the statutory regulations imposed on the water companies after they were privatised.

5

Without further ado, the tasters set to work. Their methods were indistinguishable from those used in wine tasting. A swirl of the glass, a thorough sniff, then a bit of slurping before swallowing. One or two of the tasters spat out the water, not wanting their palates to coarsen through over use. Then they compared notes.

6

This was, potentially, a laborious process. When water was privatised, nothing was left to chance and a long list of things for the tasters to look out for was produced. Did the water taste bitter? Metallic? Fishy? Oily? Did it smell soapy? Putrid? Woody? Earthy? Was there a hint of disinfectant? Was there an aroma of decayed vegetables?

7

When the marks were compared, all the tasters had given every sample a straight zero: the highest mark water can get. No smell, no taste, nothing. It had achieved the high standards Thames Water always aims for.

Part 2

You are going to read an extract from a book. For questions **8-15**, choose the answer **A**, **B**, **C** or **D** which you think fits best according to the text.

As with all hotels, the St Gregory stirred early, coming awake like a veteran combat soldier after a short, light sleep. Long before the earliest waking guest stumbled from bed to bathroom, the machinery of a new day slid quietly into motion.

Just before 5 am, night cleaning parties which for eight hours had cleaned public rooms, lower stairways, kitchen area and the reception area, wearily began to take apart their equipment, preparing to store it for another day. Behind them, floors gleamed and metalwork shone, everything giving off the pleasant odour of fresh wax.

One cleaner, old Meg Yetmein, who had worked in the hotel for thirty years, walked awkwardly. Anyone noticing her might have mistaken her clumsy walk for tiredness. The real reason, however, was a two-kilo sirloin steak taped securely to the inside of her thigh. Half an hour earlier, during a short break, Meg had snatched the steak from a kitchen fridge. From long experience she knew exactly where to look and afterwards how to conceal her prize in an old polishing rag on the way to the women's toilet. There, safe behind a locked door, she brought out some tape and fixed the steak in place. The procedure was foolproof, as she had proven many times before.

Two floors above Meg and behind an unmarked, securely locked door, a switchboard operator put down her knitting and made the first morning wake-up call. The operator was Mrs Eunice Ball, the senior of three operators who worked the night shift. Occasionally, before 7 am, the switchboard trio would wake other guests whose instructions were recorded in a card index drawer in front of them. After seven o'clock the tempo would increase.

With experienced fingers, Mrs Ball flipped through the cards. As usual, she observed, the peak would be 7.45 with nearly one hundred and eighty calls requested. Even working at high speed, the three operators would have trouble completing that many in less than twenty minutes, which meant they would have to start early, at 7.35 – assuming they had finished the 7.30 calls by then – and continue until 7.55, which would take them straight into the eight o'clock requests. Mrs Ball sighed. Inevitably there would be complaints from guests alleging that a stupid switchboard operator had called them too early or too late. One thing was good, though. Few guests at this time of the morning were in the mood for conversation or ready to flirt, the way they were at night – the reason for the locked, unmarked outer door.

Two floors below street level, in the engineering control room, Wallace Santopadre, third-class engineer, put down his book and went to check that everything was in working order. The hum of machinery greeted him as he opened the control room door. He checked the hot-water system, noting a temperature which indicated, in turn, that the time-controlled thermostat was doing its job. There would be plenty of hot water during the heavy demand period soon to come, when more than 800 people might decide to take morning baths or showers at the same time.

The massive air conditioners – twenty-five hundred tons of specialised machinery – were running more easily as a result of a drop in temperature during the night. The comparative coolness had made it possible to shut down one compressor, and now the others could be relieved alternately, allowing maintenance work which had had to be delayed during the heatwave of the previous weeks. The chief engineer, Wallace Santopadre thought, would be pleased about that.

8 Why does the writer compare the St Gregory with a veteran combat soldier?

A Combat soldiers normally sleep in beds.
B Hotels are tough, like combat soldiers.
C Combat soldiers don't rest for very long.
D The St Gregory was popular with combat soldiers.

9 What does 'it' in line 11 refer to?

A the reception area
B cleaning equipment
C the kitchen
D the cleaners' preparation

10 Why was Meg Yetmein walking awkwardly?

A She had stolen some meat.
B She was exhausted.
C She had been drinking cooking wine.
D She was rushing to the toilet.

11 What time was requested most for a wake-up call?

A 7.35 am
B 7.30 am
C 7.55 am
D 7.45 am

12 Why was the door to the room where the operators worked kept locked?

A They didn't want to be disturbed.
B They didn't want guests to complain to them.
C Their work was confidential.
D It was required by law.

13 Where was Wallace Santopadre working?

A two floors below the switchboard
B on the second floor
C on the third floor
D under ground

14 How was the water heated?

A Mr Santopadre had to open steam valves.
B It was done automatically.
C There were special heaters Mr Santopadre had to switch on.
D Steam was pumped in from another building.

15 Why hadn't the air conditioners been maintained?

A One had broken down so the others couldn't be stopped.
B The chief engineer wouldn't allow it.
C The weather had been too hot.
D They didn't have the right tools.

Part 3

You are going to read an article about dry-cleaning. Seven paragraphs have been removed from the article. Choose from the paragraphs **A-H** the one which fits each gap (**16-21**). There is one extra paragraph which you do not need to use. There is an example at the beginning (**0**).

Home and Dry

A new DIY kit claims to clean clothes 'professionally' for 65p a garment. We put it to the test in New York.

Over the years I've built up cleaning bills the size of small mortgages and destroyed my fingernails while washing by hand.

0 H

I admit to some scepticism when I tested Dryel, which the manufacturers promise will halve dry-cleaning bills by freshening up clothes between professional cleaning. The do-it-yourself kit – in a nice presentation box that looks like a Barbie doll's washing machine – offers a two-step process and incredibly simple instructions.

16 ______

My first test was to sprinkle tabasco sauce on an old blue pullover. I left it for a couple of hours to let the stain sink in and set to work on a pair of black linen trousers stained by candle wax – which professional cleaning didn't remove.

17 ______

So I didn't expect the candle wax to come out when I tried it myself. More in despair than hope, I popped the little Dryel absorbent pad under the stain as instructed, poured remover mixture onto the mark and used the tip of the bottle to rub it away. The once-sticky, caked-in blobs came off in about three minutes.

18 ______

With the stains successfully removed it was on to the next stage. It was time to get the dry-cleaning process under way.

19 ______

The manufacturers recommend you dry the bag for 30 minutes. That surprised me because the dryers in my block of flats are very hot. Twenty minutes is usually long enough to shrink my pullovers, leave singe marks on polo necks and generally destroy everything sight.

20 ______

Inside, instead of the crumpled mess I feared, two perfect pairs of trousers complete with original stiff creases down the front and a fluffy blue pullover that hadn't lost bits of wool came out.

21 ______

The manufacturers have been testing Dryel among about 150,000 consumers across America and Ireland for the past year and it goes on sale shortly. I, for one, will definitely be using it again.

A I popped the pullover, two pairs of trousers and another top I would normally handwash into the large re-usable plastic bag, put in the flowery smelling dry-cleaning cloth, sealed down the Velcro fastener and loaded it into the tumble dryer.

B It may be even cheaper. The kit itself will be priced at £10 for both the starter pack and the refill kit. I cleaned four garments in a bag in a 50p tumble dryer.

C There's a plastic bottle of stain remover and some absorbent pads to scrub away at dirty marks. Then there's a large plastic bag and fluffy pre-moistened pieces of cloth to use for the dry-cleaning itself.

D Amazed, I set to work on the mess I'd made with the tabasco sauce. It took a little longer and the liquid went a bit frothy but the pad underneath absorbed the stain. Six minutes later, there wasn't a mark left on my pullover.

E I put the machine on medium heat cycle, set the timer and crossed my fingers. Thirty minutes later I pulled the hot bag from the machine and a wonderful, newly laundered smell wafted out.

F In New York, with half a dozen dry-cleaning stores on each block, the competition is fierce and the prices keen. It cost me £6 to have the trousers dry-cleaned and, when it failed, an argument to get them cleaned again. To be fair I got them back dry-cleaned free after two days ... but still with the stain.

G Everything looks just perfect, but I wasn't completely satisfied. Just for good measure, I tried everything on. Nothing had shrunk!

H But all that is set to change thanks to a new invention that allows anyone with a tumble dryer to do what the professionals have been doing for years.

Part 4

You are going to read some information about activities to do in various locations. For questions **22-35** choose from the list of activities (**A-G**). The activities may be chosen more than once. When more than one answer is required, these may be given in any order. There is an example at the beginning (**0**).

During which activity would you

watch animals eating?	**0** B		
learn to recognise animals?	**22**		
see several geological features?	**23**		
make your own transport?	**24**		
sleep outdoors every night?	**25**	**26**	**27**
help in a scientific study?	**28**		
see the remains of an ancient civilisation?	**29**	**30**	
explore sunken ships?	**31**		
travel a very long distance over a long time?	**32**		
see beautiful shores?	**33**		
spend time in the jungle?	**34**		
pay very little to take part in an activity?	**35**		

Ways to Spend your Days of Leisure

Travellers can find thrills and spills in exotic locations

A Horse Riding

A ten-day ride through the Andean highlands in Ecuador is a fine introduction to exploring remote locations on horseback. Starting north of Quito, the trail crosses high grasslands and continues though an avenue of volcanoes. Accommodation varies from tents to local guest houses, including one next to an important archaeological Inca site.

B Volunteer Conservation

A project to study endangered orang utans in Indonesia is one of the new projects for 1999 from the Oxford-based charity, *Earthwatch*. Volunteers will be based at an orang utan rehabilitation centre in the Gunung Lower National Park in Sumatra and will go on field trips into the rainforest to observe the animals' behaviour and help with laboratory work. Much of the research involves studying how the primates feed on medicinal plants as a way of preventing parasite infection. Part of the cost of £1,150 for two weeks including food and accommodation helps fund the research.

C Diving

Dive the world's highest mountain off the Pacific island of Guam. The adjacent Marianas Trench, the world's deepest ocean gully, plunges over seven miles to the sea-bed. Guam also offers some of the best wreck diving in the world at a depth of 10-40 metres. Flights cost £450 and, once there, diving is cheap.

D Log Rafting

You're given camping equipment, plans on how to build a raft, 170 spruce logs and 460 metres of rope but no nails or hammers. Once you've built your vessel, you spend the rest of the week floating almost 100 kilometres down the Klarälven river, through the forests at about 1.5kph; stop where you want, sleep on the raft or camp on the river bank.

E Sea Kayaking

In one of the world's most magnificent stretches of coastline – the Abel Tasman National Park on the South Island – a sea kayak is a superb way of exploring the golden sandy beaches and rocky inlets, and getting close to penguins, native birds and seals. A five-day trip, camping on the beach, costs £140.

F Overland Adventure

A good idea for the lone or inexperienced adventure traveller is an overland group trip. Dragoman runs a six-month journey from the UK to Cape Town, South Africa aboard 4WD supertrucks. Highlights include the pyramids at Giza, a trip to Zanzibar and night safaris in Zambia. At Victoria Falls you can go bungee jumping, white-water rafting or canoeing.

G Living in the Bush

Conservation-based tour operator *Discovery Initiatives* offers an introduction to the life of a game warden, based in the Mpumalanga safari park adjacent to the Kruger National Park. The ten-day course covers all aspects of conservation and knowledge of safari parks, from identification and tracking to animal anatomy and handling, and camping under the stars.

Hints on writing a discursive composition

A discursive composition is one that includes some opinions and suggestions on a subject that has been presented to you by a teacher.

Approach
Logical planning is very necessary for an effective discursive composition. When you have read the question carefully, it is a good to decide what you are going to put in each paragraph.

- Introduction → this should introduce the subject briefly, but in an interesting way.
- Main Body → two or three paragraphs, each with a distinct topic sentence so the reader can immediately understand what point you are making. A new paragraph for new ideas.
- Conclusion → a short summary of the opinions you have already expressed and a brief sentence with your own personal opinion.

Pre-exam preparation
Read magazine and newspaper articles on subjects that often appear in the exam. See how the arguments are presented and supported and note down any useful idioms and expressions. Try to write your own version of the article in the form of a discursive composition and give it to your teacher for marking. Practice makes perfect!

Remember
A neutral tone is necessary in a discursive composition, so it is better to use expressions like 'Many people think...' or 'It is thought...' etc, rather than using the personal pronoun 'I'.

Part 1

You **must** answer this question.

1 You work in a hotel and the manager, who is away for a few days, has asked you to answer any enquiries. Read part of a letter you have received and the note the manager has left for you. Then write a letter, giving the sender of the letter the information required.

We would like a double room from 7th July to 16th July (9 nights) with breakfast and an evening meal.

We have been told by one of your regular guests, Ms Tanya Grey, that you organise tours during the summer. Could you please give us details of those we will be able to go on during our stay. We would also be grateful if you could send us all the relevant information about the hotel.

We look forward to hearing from you.

Yours sincerely

Jack Roberts

Jack Roberts

CORRESPONDENCE (points to include)

July bookings

- *only twin rooms and singles available from 1st to 21st (all with sea view)*
- *cost: twin £70 per night, single £50 per night (inclusive of breakfast and one meal)*
- *transfer to and from station - ask for travel details*
- *wide range of entertainment for guests, eg dance evenings*

July tours (admission included, so no extras)

1-3	Historical sites	WHOLE DAY	£25 per person
5-8	Shakespeare country	WHOLE DAY	£35 per person
10-12	Agricultural Show	HALF DAY	£15 per person
14-20	London Museums	WHOLE DAY	£45 per person
23-30	Sights of London	WHOLE DAY	£45 per person

Don't forget to thank them for their enquiry!

Write a **letter** of between **120** and **180** words in an appropriate style. Do not write any addresses.

Part 2

Write an answer to **one** of the questions **2-5** in this part. Write your answer in **120-180** words in an appropriate style.

2 You have seen this in an international magazine.

> **COMPETITION**
>
> Write and tell us what you believe makes a perfect teacher.
> The winning article will be published in this magazine and the winner will receive a prize of £1,000.

Now write your **article** for the magazine.

3 You have had a class discussion about the following statement:

Life is much easier for teenagers nowadays than it used to be.

Your teacher has now asked you to write a composition, giving your own views on the statement.

Write your **composition**.

4 This is part of a letter you receive from a pen friend.

> *I'm determined to do something about my shyness because I hate being lonely. The thing is I don't really know what to do so I was wondering if you could give me some advice about meeting people.*

Write a **letter**, giving advice to your pen friend. Do not write any addresses.

5 Background reading texts

Answer **one** of the following two questions based on your reading of **one** of the set books. Your answer should contain enough detail to make it clear to someone who may not have read the book.

Either (a) The book or the film based on the book? Write a composition, describing the parts of the book which, in your opinion, would not be as good in a film.

or (b) Some people read the same book more than once. Write a composition, giving reasons why someone would want to read the book you have read for a second time.

Hints on error correction (Part 4)

You must decide if each of the fifteen lines of a text contains an extra word or not. Most lines contain errors and they are the type of errors the FCE level learners make in their writing such as a preposition put in where there shouldn't be one.
For example:

It was about three o'clock before they reached to the top

The extra word which should not be there is 'to' because 'reach' is not followed by 'to'. You must also look at the lines before and after the one you are checking to see if the error occurs because of the structure of the previous line.
For example:

At that age it was not often that his mother let
him to go out on his own. In fact, she only ...

There is no 'extra' word in the first line but 'to' should not be in the second line because the word 'let' is used in the first.

Approach
Often the line you read doesn't sound correct but it is not immediately obvious why. Remove one word at a time until it does sound right. Do not remove a word without re-reading the line. Remember that the extra word appears in each line so you must read the whole sentence before deciding whether there is a word that should not be there.

Pre-exam Preparation
Correct your own work and that of your classmates. Pay close attention to work that has been corrected by your teacher.

Remember
Don't leave any blank spaces on your answer sheet, even when a line is correct. Don't forget you have to mark that line with a tick (✓).

Part 1

For questions **1-15**, read the text below and decide which answer **A**, **B**, **C** or **D** best fits each space. There is an example at the beginning (**0**).

Example:

0	**A** group	**B** batch	**C** pack	**D** flock

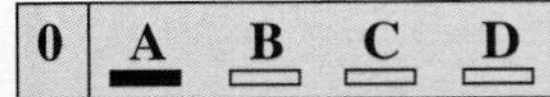

The Orkney Islands

The Orkneys are a (0) .... of seventy low, treeless islands off the north (1) .... of Scotland. Being (2) .... between the North Sea and the North Atlantic, the islands are exposed to (3) .... winds almost every day of the year, which is one of the reasons why only eighteen of them are (4) ....

Despite being a long (5) .... from a major city, the islands have a (6) .... number of archaeological sites. The Neolithic village of Skara Brae, which dates from 3100 BC and the Stones of Stenness, which are (7) .... five thousand years old are the most important of them. The most impressive building of the Orkneys is St Magnus Cathedral. This magnificent building, which is also the most expensive to (8) ...., was begun in 1137.

Today, the islanders feel closer to Norway than to Scotland. This is (9) .... the fact that the islands were (10) .... by Norsemen in the ninth century. They reigned for five hundred years before transferring them back to Scotland but left a legacy. The Orkney dialect still (11) .... several old Norse words.

(12) .... many villages, those of the Orkneys are experiencing a fall in population. The most affected island is Papa Westray with only sixty-five locals (13) .... with three hundred and thirty-seven a hundred years ago. The (14) .... of work and the fact that the islanders work the land rather than the sea make it likely that this trend will continue in the (15) .... future.

1	**A** bay	**B** shore	**C** beach	**D** coast
2	**A** located	**B** sited	**C** discovered	**D** placed
3	**A** heavy	**B** great	**C** tough	**D** high
4	**A** populated	**B** residential	**C** inhabited	**D** lived
5	**A** route	**B** path	**C** road	**D** way
6	**A** wide	**B** important	**C** large	**D** big
7	**A** above	**B** before	**C** over	**D** near
8	**A** hold	**B** maintain	**C** build	**D** keep
9	**A** due to	**B** despite	**C** since	**D** owing to
10	**A** surrendered	**B** gained	**C** beaten	**D** conquered
11	**A** consists	**B** contains	**C** keeps	**D** holds
12	**A** As	**B** For	**C** Like	**D** Similar
13	**A** compared	**B** judged	**C** estimated	**D** contrasted
14	**A** lack	**B** necessity	**C** amount	**D** need
15	**A** soon	**B** near	**C** coming	**D** short

Part 2

For questions **16-30**, read the text below and think of the word which best fits each space. Use only one word in each space. There is an example at the beginning (**0**).

The Tower of London

The Tower of London is (0) ......not........ , as the name might suggest, a single building (16) .... a number of buildings within a large stone wall.

The original building was begun in 1066. It is known (17) .... the White Tower, a name it was given after Henry III (18) .... it painted white in 1240. The White Tower was used as a royal palace by William I and many other monarchs for almost five centuries. Although it is (19) .... officially a royal palace, it has not been the main home to a monarch since Henry VIII died in 1509. (20) .... the first building was completed, monarchs who followed added buildings and (21) .... them for different purposes.

(22) .... the late 1200s to the end of the eighteenth century coins were made (23) .... It was first used as a zoo during the reign of Henry III and remained one (24) .... 1835, when the animals were moved to the new London Zoo. As (25) .... as being a mint and a zoo, it was a prison. It was 'home' to several historical figures, a (26) .... of whom were executed.

Today, it is a major tourist attraction. Visitors can (27) .... the crown jewels, which have been kept at the Tower since the seventeenth century. (28) .... highlight of the tour is the ravens – big black birds which live there permanently. According (29) .... legend, the British crown will never fall (30) .... the ravens leave.

Part 3

For questions **31-40**, complete the second sentence so that it has a similar meaning to the first sentence, using the word given. **Do not change the word given.** You must use between two and five words including the word given. There is an example at the beginning (**0**).

0 Having an argument with your boss is the last thing I would do.
idea
It wouldn't be .... an argument with your boss.

The gap can be filled by the words 'a good idea to have' so you write:

0	*a good idea to have*

31 It was her first parachute jump.
time
It was .... made a parachute jump.

32 As it was raining heavily, we decided to stay in.
because
We decided to stay in .... rain.

33 It's a pity Lesley and I fell out.
wish
I .... out with Lesley.

34 This watch is yours, isn't it?
belongs
This watch .... it?

35 "I know you can try harder, Millie," said her father.
accused
Millie's father .... hard enough.

36 They finished the job very quickly.
take
It .... to finish the job.

37 Bringing all these pullovers was completely unnecessary.
have
We .... all these pullovers.

38 It's common knowledge that Philip broke the law on several occasions.
known
Philip .... the law on several occasions.

39 Alec can't build his house without getting permission from the Town Hall.
gets
Alec can't build his house .... permission from the Town Hall.

40 Judy was the only one who answered the question correctly.
apart
Everyone got the answer .... Judy.

Part 4

For questions **41-55**, read the text below and look carefully at each line. Some of the lines are correct and some have a word which should not be there. If a line is correct put a tick (✓) by the number. If a line has a word which should not be there, write the word. There are two examples at the beginning (**0** and **00**).

An Eye-catching Car

0 Not so long ago I had the good fortune to make friends
00 with a neighbour who was owned a garage which specialised in
41 repairing quality cars. He usually arrived at home with a customer's
42 car when he finished work in order to test it all fully before
43 giving it back the following day. Most of the cars he has brought
44 back were more expensive but I didn't really like them. That was
45 until one day when I saw a Daimler 5.3 parked outside of his
46 house. At that time such a car was cost about £30.000. This
47 meant that I could only to dream of owning or driving
48 one. After a moment's hesitation, I knocked on his door and
49 waited. When he answered, I was staring at the car so he
50 knew about what I was going to ask him. He invited me in
51 for a cup of some tea and tried to tell me that driving the
52 car was out of the question. However, this did not put me off
53 and I eventually managed to persuade him to let me to drive
54 it. The experience was very incredible. The car was powerful,
55 quiet and extremely comfortable. The only problem was that my own
car seemed terribly disappointing when I drove it later that evening.

0	✓
00	*was*
41	
42	
43	
44	
45	
46	
47	
48	
49	
50	
51	
52	
53	
54	
55	

Part 5

For questions **56-65**, read the text below. Use the word given in capitals at the end of each line to form a word that fits in the space in the same line. There is an example at the beginning (**0**).

Danger in the Water

It is common (0) ....knowledge...... that swimming in the sea, especially in	KNOW
(56) .... waters can be dangerous. Now, however, bathers in the	TROPICS
cooler seas around Britain have made the (57) .... that	DISCOVER
swimming or paddling in the comparative (58) .... of the seas	SAFE
off British coasts can be a (59) .... business. The danger exists	RISK
in the form of the weaver fish, whose (60) .... sting can cause	PAIN
potentially fatal allergic (61) .... in young children and can	REACT
further (62) .... the heart of an elderly person. When the	WEAK
weaver fish uses its sting, it is not behaving (63) .... but merely	AGGRESSION
acting defensively since the (64) .... of a large foot descending	SEE
is perceived as a threat. (65) .... for the majority the sting can	FORTUNE
be easily treated by soaking it in hot water.	

Extension and Revision

A Vocabulary Building

Complete the unfinished words in the following sentences. The words are all related to the media.

1 Did they broad.................. the match live or was it re.................. ?
2 Are you sure that the fre.................. you gave me for the local radio st.................. was correct?
3 This newspaper has a circ.................. of over three million!
4 It's an interesting news it.................. but I don't think it'll make the head..................
5 The ed.................. is responsible for the art.................. that make up a newspaper.
6 Without a sat.................. dish, you won't be able to tu.................. into that cha.................. very well.
7 There's nothing wrong with the aer .... It's just that the rec .... isn't very good in this area.
8 Her uncle is a jour.................. for a local paper and her aunt is a war corr.................. for a national TV station.
9 He writes a gos.................. col.................. for a national daily.
10 Which sec.................. of the newspaper do you read first?

B Word Use

Use the words on the left to complete the sentences on the right. Make sure the word is in the correct form.

1 **bay**, **shore**, **beach**, **coast**

a There's nothing like sunbathing on a sandy ....
b The weather forecast said there would be strong winds off the east ....
c At night you can see the lights from fishing boats in the ....
d It was rather silly of them to go to sea without a ship to .... radio.

2 **route**, **path**, **way**

a I think you've gone the wrong .... I don't remember this road.
b We walked along a narrow .... through the forest.
c They always go to work by the same ....

3 **surrender**, **gain**, **beat**, **conquer**

a They .... only when there was no hope of escape.
b It took him years to .... his fear of the dark.
c What do you hope to .... by insulting her
d We went on holiday early in order to .... the crowds.

4 **consist**, **contain**, **hold**

a The petrol can will .... about ten litres.
b His 'security system' .... of a steel door and two large dogs.
c One of the boxes we found .... some old photographs.

5 **lack**, **necessity**, **need**

a We couldn't work together due to a .... of cooperation.
b There was no .... to shout at him.
c Unless you consider it a .... , we won't buy it.

C Use of Prepositions

Use the prepositions below to complete the sentences which follow.

about at for in of on with (x2)

1 Our librarian will provide you .... all the information you need.
2 Gordon accused me .... lying to him.
3 She has a special relationship .... her aunt.
4 You can't blame anyone but yourself .... your mistakes.
5 It's unkind to laugh .... people less fortunate than you.
6 I met her .... my way to work last Monday.
7 You should complain to the manager .... this food.
8 Tom was .... a surprisingly good mood this morning.

D Word Formation

I Use the word in capitals at the end of each sentence to form a word that fits in the space in the sentence.

1	The bridge was .... during the earthquake.	WEAK
2	.... , the fireman was able to rescue the child.	FORTUNE
3	I wouldn't like to travel long distances in this car because the seats are	COMFORT
4	Sparing no thought for her own .... , she dived into the river to save the child.	SAFE
5	Animals react .... if other animals invade their territory.	AGGRESSION

II Choose the odd word out from the following groups of words according to how they form adjectives.

1	grow	disgust	react	win
2	fault	space	silk	fun
3	appear	obey	accept	depend
4	threat	rot	freeze	swell
5	rest	self	fool	Britain
6	end	point	home	forget

Hints on how to select from 2 or 3 possible answers (Part 4)

In part 4 of the listening exam you will come across one of three possible question types:

- multiple-choice (usually A, B or C)
- true/false OR yes/no (in other words, two choices)
- multiple matching

You are probably more familiar with the first two. Multiple matching, however, needs a little bit of attention. You may be asked to choose any one of the following combinations:

- choose from three options (eg Which garden has this?: Garden A, Garden B or Garden C?)
- choose from one option, another option or both (eg Which person says this?: Person A, Person B or both people?)
- choose from one option, another option or neither (Which magazine states this?: Magazine A, Magazine B or neither magazine?)

Approach
The most important aspect in this part of the exam is to read your questions properly. You are given a whole minute to read through before you start. Listen very carefully to the details and make sure that the items you select really do match what the question has asked you. Really concentrate on understanding in detail what each speaker says.

Pre-exam preparation
Listen to news broadcasts on radio or TV as much as possible. At first, it might be difficult to catch all the details, but with practice you should be able to listen to and summarise the main points of each news item.

Remember
Make sure you transfer your answers to the special answer sheet accurately and clearly. Check that you mark the right choice next to the appropriate question number and that you don't jump a line.

Part 1

You will hear people talking in eight different situations. For questions **1-8**, choose the best answer, **A**, **B** or **C**.

1 A guest speaker is being introduced at a social club. Why is the guest speaker famous?

A He is a great artist.
B He is an actor.
C He is a professional sportsman.

2 You hear part of a recipe being read out on a radio show. What is the recipe for?

A a pie
B a cake
C a main course

3 You hear a representative talking at an exhibition. What is the main advantage of the boat he is trying to sell?

A It is faster than others of the same type.
B It is the cheapest in its class.
C It is tougher than others of the same type.

4 You hear two classmates talking about their school reports. How do they feel?

A satisfied
B disappointed
C very pleased

5 You hear two people talking about a holiday. Why was the woman disappointed?

A The hotel was too noisy.
B The weather wasn't very good.
C She found the meals at the hotel awful.

6 You hear two English tourists speaking to each other. What does the woman suggest?

A that the man should fly home immediately
B that the man should wait and see if he gets better
C that the man should make enquiries elsewhere

7 You hear two people talking about primary schools. What does the woman think is responsible for the change in pupils' behaviour?

A Most primary school teachers used to be old.
B The situation in many homes is different now.
C Naughty children no longer get beaten.

8 You hear a customer talking to a shop assistant. Why is she complaining?

A The scarf has a stain on it.
B The scarf has a hole in it.
C The scarf is not exactly the same colour as she wanted.

Part 2

You will hear a telephone conversation about a meeting. For questions **9-18**, complete the notes made by Tanya. You will need to write a word, short phrase or number in each box.

MEETING IN LONDON

Held at [9]

Time of meeting [10]

Not enough copies of report. Make an extra [11]

Travel:

Going by [12]

Departs at [13]

From platform [14]

Meet by [15]

Gets in at [16]

From station to meeting [17]

Talk: (not to include sales)

New Title: [18]

Part 3

You will hear five different people talking about their business. For questions **19-23**, choose which of the people **A-F** is speaking. Use the letters only once. There is one extra letter which you do not need to use.

A a florist

B a carpenter

C a jeweller

D an optician

E a greengrocer

F a designer

Speaker 1		**19**
Speaker 2		**20**
Speaker 3		**21**
Speaker 4		**22**
Speaker 5		**23**

Part 4

You will hear part of a radio interview about dolphins. For questions **24-30**, choose the best answer **A**, **B** or **C**.

24 The dolphin's and porpoise's closest relative is

A the shark.
B the tuna fish.
C the whale.

24

25 Dolphins cannot understand

A spoken orders.
B visual signals.
C written instructions.

25

26 Dolphins' behaviour

A can vary from school to school.
B is never the same in any two schools.
C seems strange when compared to that of other animals.

26

27 Dolphins receive messages

A through their forehead.
B through the bottom part of their mouth.
C in their inner ear.

27

28 The Ganges River Dolphin is dying out because

A new diseases have been killing them.
B people are breaking the law.
C there is too much pollution where they live.

28

29 The pressure put on countries to stop using illegal nets

A has caused problems between nations.
B has led to fewer dolphins being killed.
C means that the survival of dolphins is guaranteed.

29

30 The dolphins in the rescue story

A carried the two Colombians on their backs.
B swam in circles round the sharks.
C kept the sharks away from the two Colombians.

30

Hints on speaking with a partner and the interlocutor

The final part of the speaking test allows you to discuss in more depth something related to the theme of Part 3 of the exam. You are expected to speak to your partner and the interlocutor, exchanging and justifying opinions.

Approach
Make sure you maintain eye contact with both people you are speaking to (just focusing on the examiner or your partner is not accurate). Try to speak as naturally as possible, as if you were with a group of friends. Don't try to dominate the conversation, but don't be too shy, either. Encourage your partner to speak if he/she does not seem to know what to say next. Qualify your opinions. Don't just say 'TV has a bad influence on young kids.' Instead, say 'TV has a bad influence on young kids, because there are many programmes that show violence as being natural and OK. My younger brother, for example, ...'.

Pre-exam preparation
Try to get as much practice speaking in English. Take every opportunity to speak inside the classroom and outside. If you have the opportunity to travel abroad, you are bound to find other foreign students who are also willing to speak in English. The more practice you get, the more you will feel at home with the language.

Remember
You will be marked on grammar, vocabulary, pronunciation, discourse management (how well you organise what you say) and interactive communication (how well you can converse). If you are too quiet, the examiner won't be able to assess you properly.

Paper 5: Speaking

Part 1 (About 3 minutes)

Ask and answer the following questions with a partner.

- Do you have any hobbies?
- How did you become interested in it/them?
- Which do you prefer more, watching TV or going to the cinema?
- What sort of programmes or films do you like to watch?
- What was the last film you saw at the cinema (or on TV)?

Part 2 (About 4 minutes)

Practise speaking about the photographs shown on page 181.

Candidate A, here are your two photographs. They show two different ways that we pollute the environment. Please let Candidate B have a look at them. Candidate A, I'd like you to compare and contrast these photographs, saying what the differences are in the way we can prevent these problems (approximately 1 minute).

Candidate B, could you please tell us which of these problems, in your opinion, causes the biggest threat to our health (approximately twenty seconds).

Candidate B, here are your two photographs. They show people with unusual jobs. Please let Candidate A have a look at them. Candidate B, I'd like you to compare and contrast these two photographs, saying what dangers these people face (approximately one minute).

Candidate A, could you please tell us which of these jobs you would prefer to do (approximately twenty seconds).

Part 3 (About 3 minutes)

Discuss the following with a partner.

Imagine your family has joined *Homeswap*, an organisation which arranges for families to exchange their homes during the holidays. Talk to each other about which three homes shown on the opposite page you would be prepared to exchange for your own and which one you would be least likely to accept. It is not necessary to agree with each other.

Part 4 (About 4 minutes)

Give each other your opinions about the following questions.

- How does where you live affect your way of life?
- What do you need to consider before you move house?
- What are the advantages of spending your whole life in one house?
- How important is the decoration in a house?
- What dangers do people face in their own homes?

Hints on improving your reading skills I

By now you are very familiar with the reading paper and the different tasks you will be expected to complete in the exam. Therefore, you are now in a position to 'polish up' your reading skills to guarantee a successful result.

Important factors regarding reading

Speed
We read much faster in our own language than in the foreign language we are learning. The exam is designed for the average student with approximately 1,900-2,300 words to be read and processed within 75 minutes. If you are already a fast reader, then there is no problem. However, if you feel that the reading paper presents you with a challenge, it is probably because you need to increase your reading speed. This does not mean that you should read so fast that you don't understand anything! The average English-speaking person may read about 300 wpm (words per minute) comfortably, whereas the average FCE student may read about 120-150 wpm with adequate comprehension. With practice this can be improved – but it means you should be reading more (and not just what is given to you by your teacher).

Flexibility
A person reading in their first language will vary their reading speed depending on several factors: the level of difficulty of the text, the reason the text is being read, and the enjoyment factor! In the exam, you will not have to read every single word in order to pass with flying colours. Your speed of reading will vary according to the task you have in front of you. You will use two particular skills:

- **scanning**: reading through very quickly to get a general impression of the text and to search for specific information
- **skimming**: glancing rapidly through the text to understand the gist

Ask yourself a question: 'Do I read everything in my own language with the same intensity and comprehension?' We are sure the answer is 'No'!

Pre-exam preparation

- Set yourself a target to read a certain amount of magazines, newspapers, comics, etc in English every month (for example, you could buy one magazine and read one article every two days).
- Get hold of material which is easy to read (never mind if it is below the level of the FCE) to start with. When you become a more confident reader, you can continue with more difficult texts. (Graded readers are good because you know the approximate level before you start.)
- When you are reading more difficult material DO NOT FEEL GUILTY for skipping unknown words – just read for enjoyment and global understanding until you gain more experience in the language.

Part 1

You are going to read a magazine article about yoga. Choose from the list (**A-I**) the sentence which best summarises each part (**1-7**) of the article. There is one extra sentence which you do not need to use. There is an example at the beginning (**0**).

A It is necessary to concentrate in order to practise yoga successfully.

B Yoga is often practised by people who are unable to do sports.

C The principle of yoga is to shut out the outside world.

D All forms of yoga share common aims.

E Yoga has caught on because it provides both mental and physical exercise.

F Yoga brings immediate results and soon becomes a way of life.

G Yoga can help to deal with health problems.

H As a form of exercise, yoga is unique in what it can achieve.

I Yoga has a new image which makes it suitable for everyone.

Stretch Yourself with Yoga

0 I

If you are fed up with step classes, have had enough of aerobics and can't stand the thought of lifting weights but still want a toned body, consider yoga. No longer associated with a group of people sitting in circles humming, modern yoga comes in a variety of forms to suit every body and need.

1

'Yoga is becoming very popular with people who want a form of exercise that works the mind and body,' explains Vimla Lalvani, one of Britain's leading yoga teachers and authors. And now that yoga has become so popular different forms of the discipline have become available in classes up and down the country.

2

Catriona Brokenshire, who teaches at the *Life Centre* in London's Notting Hill, explains its popularity: 'If you want a body that is strong and supple but in harmony and balanced, then yoga is for you. If you're sluggish, it gives you energy; if you're hyper, it can calm you. No other exercise regime can offer those benefits.'

3

Catriona teaches Astanga Vinyassa, or 'power yoga', which is favoured by celebrities including Madonna and Ralph Fiennes. But she is keen to explain that no matter which form of yoga you try, all are firmly based on the same principles and similar movements. 'All systems of yoga are essentially the same. They see the body as a vehicle for the spirit, while stretching the muscles, focusing the thoughts and guiding the breathing.'

4

And it's not just your body that can reap the benefits, but your health, too. Recent clinical trials have shown that yoga can assist in the management of anxiety, asthma, heart disease, mild forms of diabetes, back pain and migraine. At the same time, people are discovering that yoga can combat fatigue.

5

But if you are looking for a form of exercise that you can simply switch off and do, yoga may not be for you, because it requires mental as well as physical concentration. 'An essential part of yoga is how you breath. Breathing affects everything – the mind, stomach, concentration, energy levels, consciousness and state of mind,' explains Catriona.

6

'Although yoga takes a lot of concentration, it is ultimately stress-relieving because you focus on yourself, not the other people in the class, your problems or the world around you,' explains Catriona. 'Yoga is not about competition or pushing yourself to the limits. It's about working with your own capacities to achieve your own goals.'

7

If you are a beginner to yoga, Catriona recommends that you start with a course of lessons, twice a week for a minimum of three months. 'You should reap the benefits straight away,' she says, 'but will really appreciate the effect after three months. By then, most people are hooked and can't imagine living without yoga.'

Part 2

You are going to read an article about a scientific development. For questions **8-14**, choose the answer **A**, **B**, **C** or **D** which you think fits best according to the text.

Let There be Light!

A German inventor creates a contact lens that could give humans eyesight as acute as a cat's

It's the 24th Century and aboard the *USS Enterprise*, *Star Trek* chief engineer Geordi La Forge scans the heavens by means of sophisticated lenses that gives him superhuman vision. That may be science fiction, but we may not have to wait 300 years before we can boldly see where no one has seen before. A new high-performance contact lens under development in the department of applied physics at the University of Heidelberg will not only correct ordinary vision defects but will improve normal night vision as much as five times, making people's vision sharper than that of cats and owls. In short, the lenses enhance vision so well that the wearer's sight is actually better than nature's perfect 20-20.

Josef Bille, a 54-year-old physics professor, and his colleagues at the university hope that their invention will enable campers to pitch their tents without torches, drivers to make out the road ahead more easily and people suffering from night blindness to see in the dark. Theatregoers might also benefit. The lenses work best when the pupils are fully dilated, as when looking at a stage from the depths of a dark auditorium. 'Forget opera glasses, says Bille, 'they will no longer be necessary.'

By day, the contact lenses will focus rays of light so accurately on the retina that the image of a small leaf or the silhouette of a distant tree will be formed with a sharpness that is far better than that of normal vision aids by almost half a dioptre – a unit of measure of the power of the lens. At night, the lenses have even greater potential. Because the new lens – in contrast to the already existing ones – also works when it's dark and the pupils are wide open. Lens wearers will be able to identify a face at a distance of 100 metres – 80 metres further than they would normally be able to see. In recent experiments night vision was improved by an even greater factor: in semi-darkness, test subjects could see up to fifteen times better than without the lenses.

Those who stand to benefit most from Bille's work are the millions who suffer from deficiencies in night vision. Wearing super lenses will put an end to nerve-racking night-time road trips, where the road ahead is hidden by impenetrable darkness and the headlights of oncoming cars painfully dazzle the eyes. 'The lenses should increase traffic safety immensely,' predicts Bille – not a small promise since accident rates can increase as much as two to three times in half-light and darkness.

Not everyone is enthusiastic, though. Dr Mehrle doesn't believe people need to have eyes like a cat because he doesn't believe there is any practical value in doing so. On the contrary, he believes that people will drive less cautiously if they can see better at night. They will increase speed and there will be just as many accidents as there are at present.

Bille's lenses are expected to reach the market in the next few years and the demand will probably be great. For members of professions in which perfect vision is a must – such as pilots or surgeons – the scientist plans to develop a special device which will adjust sight to the best possible degree at every given moment. Bille himself will be the first to benefit from the super lenses. At the moment he is extremely short-sighted and wears very thick glasses.

8 What will the new lenses do?

A They will work like normal glasses or contact lenses.
B They will only improve night vision.
C They will allow people to see far better than normal.
D They will cure a person's eyes of all their problems.

9 When do the lenses work best?

A when the wearer uses a torch
B when there isn't much light round the wearer
C when the wearer is driving
D when they are worn together with glasses

10 What does 'that' in line 32 refer to?

A a silhouette
B a small leaf
C a measure of the power of a lens
D sharpness

11 According to Bille, how will the lenses help drivers?

A There will be fewer accidents.
B They will allow new traffic safety measures to be taken.
C They will help learners pass the driving test.
D They will stop drivers from becoming nervous.

12 Why does Dr Mehrle think the lenses aren't useful?

A People will drive faster when they use them.
B They will cause the wearer to become dependent on them.
C Their benefits are only temporary.
D They are not practical.

13 What is likely to happen when the lenses go on sale?

A They will be quite expensive at first.
B They will sell very well.
C They will only be available in certain areas.
D Customers will have to order them through an optician.

14 How will the lenses worn by pilots or surgeons be better?

A They will always allow the wearer to see as well as possible.
B They will be made of a more expensive material.
C They will be able to adjust at the touch of a button.
D They will be unbreakable and made of thick material.

Part 3

You are going to read an article about honey. Eight sentences have been removed from the article. Choose from the sentences **A-I** the one which fits each gap (**15-21**). There is one extra sentence which you do not need to use. There is an example at the beginning (**0**).

Honey, Food of the Centuries

Of all naturally occurring foods, honey is the one that seems to hold the most magic and mystery. **0** I The beekeeper must simply cross his fingers and hope.

The queen bee appears to have an easy life. Once mated, she returns to the hive to live a life of pampered luxury, sipping royal jelly and laying eggs. **15** ____ Fortunately, they are so good at this and so driven in their work that they make an enormous excess of honey, and it is harvested twice a year.

The colour, flavour and density of honey depends entirely on which flowers the bees visit. **16** ____ As regards smell, some honeys are scentless while wildflower honey has a heady perfume.

17 ____ Highly scented but not too sweet, it has an almost jelly-like texture and is tasty spread on fresh bread with butter.

Mexican blossom honey, clear and dark with an almost sharp flavour is best kept for creamy desserts. Acacia honey, mildly sweet with floral overtones, goes well with yoghurt or porridge. **18** ____ It is best brushed on to the skin of roast duck about twenty minutes before the bird is removed from the oven.

The texture of honey depends on how the fruit sugars are mixed. **19** ____ If you prefer clear honey simply warm set honey before use. I love the rough uneven crunch of crystallised honey.

20 ____ It was one of the few sweeteners available in cold northern countries, where sweet fruit, such as figs, raisins and dates, were costly imports.

This year the first national honey week takes place. It has been organised to encourage people to enjoy this delicious, healthy food so look out for a new or unusual jar of honey and take it home. **21** ____

A Those with a high glucose content, such as rape flower, crystallise easily but acacia, which has a higher fructose level, is clear.

B It might have a wonderful effect on you.

C Heather honey is the most delicious.

D Honey keeps for centuries if stored in a cool, dry place and has been found in good condition in the tombs of Egyptian Pharaohs.

E It is easy to see why honey was important and popular before the arrival of white sugar.

F It is the lesser bees that do all the real work, collecting nectar which is then made into honey as food for the hive.

G Dark amber Greek honey is highly recommended in cooking.

H Colours range from white, through brilliant yellow, to deep, dark gold.

I Though apiculturists can keep their bees in optimum conditions and breed queens with good genetic lines, the collection of pollen and nectar is beyond human control.

Part 4

You are going to read seven extracts about different aspects of natural disasters. For questions **22-35**, choose from the extracts **A-G**. The extracts may be chosen more than once. There is an example at the beginning (**0**).

Which person says:

dangers are always present?	0	A
technology is helping to predict disasters?	22	
disasters can lead to crime?	23	
money can't help you recover completely?	24	
lack of preparation can be fatal?	25	
more people live in high-risk areas?	26	
soldiers prevented lawlessness?	27	
we mistakenly believe we can deal with disasters?	28	
new warning devices could save lives?	29	
you have to start all over again after a disaster?	30, 31	
the relief agency was better than expected?	32	
coping with a second disaster is easier?	33	
there's no evidence disasters occur much more frequently?	34	
a disaster makes you appreciate what you had before?	35	

Natural Disasters

A Michael Parfit, writer

We are surrounded by many dangers. Much of the time we appear to have them under control, but the measures we take sometimes wrongly give us the impression of security. However, disasters seem to be hitting us harder and harder. In the US the cost of natural disasters now stands at about £50 billion a year.

B Chris Tucker, scientific adviser

I can show you figures which indicate that the costs of natural disasters are going up rapidly, but I can't prove that meteorological events have become more common. Many people argue that the increase in urban populations in dangerous areas is responsible.

C Tod DeMilly, former mayor

After Hurricane Andrew hit Homestead, Florida, the really bad side of some people came out. These were mostly people who came in to steal. But we also had mothers who had no food for their babies stealing for survival. We couldn't arrest them because we had nowhere to put them. It was chaos. For a while, Homestead was like the Wild West, with armed homeowners wandering the streets. Then the army came in and things settled down.

D Sander Halet, tornado survivor

You get to a point where you're OK and so is your family. You're not injured and you're not going to die of starvation but you've got to rebuild your life. It makes you realise how lucky you were before. I went to the Red Cross to see if they could help. I was surprised at how well they have everything planned. Their concern gave me hope and made me think ahead.

E Peter O'Neill, scientist

It might help if predictions became more accurate and in many ways things are improving. Meteorologists at the National Hurricane Centre, armed with aircraft, satellites and computers claim an increase in forecast accuracy of one per cent. Researchers are also developing electronic warning systems that could race ahead of an earthquake, giving nearby communities up to a minute to get ready – at least enough time to seek shelter.

F Freda Samuel, relief agency worker

Preparation is the reason why so many of us get through significant hazards almost routinely. Mexicans live comfortably in heat that could kill in Toronto, but when temperatures in Mexico fell to the level of a mild Canadian winter, thousands of Mexicans were unprepared and dozens died.

G Eliza Perry, disaster survivor

How do you put everything back together? You don't, you build something different. You may get financial help but that doesn't repair your spirit. That's a part of dealing with a disaster that you have to manage on your own. If you cope successfully, then a disaster won't hit you so hard the next time.

Hints on writing a short story

You may choose to write a narrative (a story) where you have to start or begin with certain words that are given to you.

Approach

- First of all, make sure that you read the instructions carefully. Do you have to begin with the given words, or do you have to end with them, or can you choose?
- Secondly, do NOT change the words you have been given – and check any pronouns carefully. If you are given the words 'He opened the letter and fainted', you cannot suddenly write about a girl called Sarah!!
- Thirdly, plan your story line before writing. If you expect the story to just 'come', then your writing will not be well organised and you are likely to run out of words before you reach a proper conclusion.
- Finally, do not be afraid to use your imagination and show the examiner that you know a wide range of vocabulary. You will also be expected to vary your tenses successfully to show a movement of time in your story.

Pre-exam preparation
Practise planning stories with a good introduction, a few details for the main body of the story and an interesting conclusion. You can look at past exam papers for example questions.

Remember
Write a story that YOU would personally like to read!

Part 1

You **must** answer this question.

1 You are going to study in England next year and you are looking for a flat to rent. Read the advertisement you saw in a newspaper and the notes you made below about your requirements. Then write a letter to *Homefinders Extra*, giving details of the kind of flat you would like to rent.

HOMEFINDERS EXTRA

Want to rent a home?

We'll do the searching for you anywhere in Britain.

Just write to: *Brian James, Lang House, Milton Common, Oxon, OX9 2JY (minimum rental 1 yr)*

FLAT

SIZE	–	1 bed, living room or studio flat
FACILITIES	–	central heating!! fully furnished + phone + TV + space for cooking
LOCATION	–	London (preferably south) maximum 30 mins from London School of Economics, good views (high floor), near park (safe jogging)
PRICE	–	£800 per month – no more!!
RENTAL	–	12 months from 1st October

Write a **letter** of between **120** and **180** words in an appropriate style. Do not write any addresses.

Part 2

Write an answer to **one** of the questions **2-5** in this part. Write your answer in **120-180** words in an appropriate style.

2 You have had a class discussion on the following question:

Should people tell the truth all the time?

Now your teacher has asked you to write a composition, giving your opinion on this question. Write your **composition**.

3 You have decided to enter a short story competition. The competition rules say that the story must begin or end with the following sentence:

I opened the box only to find that it was completely empty.

Write your **story** for the competition.

4 Your penfriend's father is a travel agent and he would like to organise a tour of your area. He wants you to help by writing a report, answering these questions:

- Which is the best hotel to stay in and why?
- Which sights should they visit and what can they see there?
- What entertainment is there in the area?

Write your **report**.

5 Background reading texts

Answer **one** of the following two questions based on your reading of **one** of the set books. Your answer should contain enough detail to make it clear to someone who may not have read the book.

Either **(a)** Which parts of the book are the most important? Write a composition, describing the most important parts and explaining why they are so important.

or **(b)** A successful book must have a good beginning and a good ending. Which was better in the book you have read? Write a composition, giving your views.

Hints on word formation

You must complete a text with ten gaps by building words from those which accompany the text. This tests the addition of affixes (comfort – uncomfortable), internal changes (sell – sale) and compounding (teen – teenager).

Approach

Look at the gap to be filled and decide what part of speech is required to fill it. Then add the necessary prefix or suffix and make any other changes necessary. Check that the meaning is correct or whether it needs a negative prefix. Check that nouns are plural when necessary (noun-verb agreement) and that verbs are in the correct form (base form, gerund, present or past participle). Read through the text and make sure it makes sense. Check your spelling carefully.

Pre-exam preparation

Adopt a systematic and methodical approach to different types of word formation.

Part 1

For questions **1-15**, read the text below and decide which answer **A**, **B**, **C** or **D** best fits each space. There is an example at the beginning (**0**).

Example:

0 **A** became **B** happened **C** came **D** remained

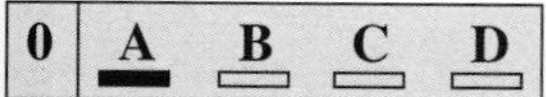

The Public Gets What the Public Wants

When it (0) .... quite (1) .... for people to own a television in the USA in the 1950s, producers were forced to (2) .... up with different kinds of programmes. One type that rapidly (3) .... popularity was the 'game show', in which contestants had to answer questions. One (4) .... programme, which was the subject of a film called *Quiz Show*, caused a scandal of nationwide proportions over forty years ago.

Like all commercial television stations, the one that (5) .... this show was interested in the number and opinions of (6) .... who watched the programme (7) ...., the sponsors were paying a great deal of money to get their (8) .... advertised. This put pressure on the producers. They had to make sure people (9) .... on watching so they carried out surveys about the contestants who (10) .... on the show. When the public grew (11) .... of the champion, there was a danger of people watching another television (12) .... which, in turn, would put their jobs (13) .... risk.

In order to keep everybody happy, they had to 'fix' the show. They did this by giving either the champion or the challenger the answers to the questions, (14) .... the public's preferences and wishes. The plan worked well for a while, but when it was (15) ...., the popularity of game shows decreased.

1	**A**	common	**B**	ordinary	**C**	frequent	**D**	regular
2	**A**	find	**B**	get	**C**	think	**D**	come
3	**A**	won	**B**	earned	**C**	took	**D**	gained
4	**A**	example	**B**	type	**C**	such	**D**	sort
5	**A**	sent	**B**	broadcast	**C**	announced	**D**	spread
6	**A**	viewers	**B**	listeners	**C**	audience	**D**	spectators
7	**A**	To sum up	**B**	In total	**C**	After all	**D**	In fact
8	**A**	stock	**B**	items	**C**	products	**D**	commodities
9	**A**	carried	**B**	insisted	**C**	stayed	**D**	kept
10	**A**	participated	**B**	appeared	**C**	contested	**D**	opposed
11	**A**	tired	**B**	bored	**C**	sick	**D**	fed up
12	**A**	canal	**B**	side	**C**	channel	**D**	station
13	**A**	in	**B**	at	**C**	to	**D**	with
14	**A**	owing to	**B**	according to	**C**	on account of	**D**	as regards
15	**A**	found	**B**	realised	**C**	discovered	**D**	understood

Part 2

For questions **16-30**, read the text below and think of the word which best fits each space. Use only one word in each space. There is an example at the beginning (**0**).

Glass

Perhaps (0) ....*one*................ of the commonest man-made substances is glass. In fact, it is (16) .... common that few people appreciate its unique qualities. Glass is (17) .... hard and transparent. It does not expand when heated, it is a very poor conductor and it is resistant to all acids (18) .... hydrofluoric acid, which dissolves it.

(19) .... knows exactly where or when the manufacture of glass began. (20) .... is known, though, is that there were skilled glass makers in ancient Egypt who practised it as (21) .... as 2000 BC, if not earlier. The Romans are also known to (22) .... been particularly good (23) .... making glass.

Glass is (24) .... from sand, an alkali and other ingredients which can (25) .... colour it or change its properties. These changes are usually achieved (26) .... adding certain chemicals during the process or placing thin layers of other substances (27) .... two sheets of glass. The nature of the glass produced also depends (28) .... the quality of the ingredients used.

Nowadays, one of the main uses of glass is in windows, which to us would seem to (29) .... quite logical. However, the art of making glass was known long (30) .... it was considered suitable for windows.

Part 3

For questions **31-40**, complete the second sentence so that it has a similar meaning to the first sentence, using the word given. **Do not change the word given**. You must use between two and five words including the word given. There is an example at the beginning (**0**).

0 He stands a very good chance of getting the job.
likely

He .... the job.

The gap can be filled by the words 'is likely to get' so you write:

0	*is likely to get*

31 Your brakes aren't working properly.
time

It .... your brakes repaired.

32 I find it surprising that Ralph didn't fail his driving test.
managed

I don't know .... his driving test.

33 I'll finish typing these letters and then I'll help you.
soon

I'll help you .... typing these letters.

34 My cousin is better at painting than I am.
as

I can't .... my cousin.

35 Why should she borrow the money from me?
reason

Give me one good .... her the money.

36 The lift has broken down yet again!
order

The lift .... yet again!

37 Make sure you have some petrol left.
run

Make sure you .... petrol.

38 Why wasn't I told about the changes?
anyone

Why .... about the changes?

39 "Do you know what has been taken, sir," asked the detective.
if

The detective asked the man .... been taken.

40 In my opinion, it's better to talk calmly than to argue.
prefer

I .... an argument.

Part 4

For questions **41-55**, read the text below and look carefully at each line. Some of the lines are correct and some have a word which should not be there. If a line is correct put a tick (✓) by the number. If a line has a word which should not be there, write the word. There are two examples at the beginning (**0** and **00**).

Some Marvellous News

0 Nowadays when it is becoming increasingly difficult to get a
00 job and people are finding it more harder to make ends meet, cash
41 prizes in lots competitions appear to be getting bigger and bigger.
42 Recently the winner of a draw which organised by a national daily
43 newspaper was announced. He was an eighteen-year-old and his own prize
44 was £50,000 a year for life! Jonathan Ring had just finished work at his
45 part-time job, for which he earns just £36 a week, when he received
46 the news that he had won the draw. At first really he couldn't
47 believe in his ears. Actually he got rather angry and asked his
48 parents to stop joking but when he saw how much serious they were,
49 he realised they were telling all the truth. Since the marvellous
50 surprise both he and his family have been planning what to do with
51 the money. He intends to go on holiday to Barbados, buy a new car
52 for his father and get a season ticket for his most favourite football
53 team. Despite of the fact that he won a large sum of money,
54 Jonathan did not celebrate with champagne but with a cup of tea.
55 He also stated that he would be continue working part-time until he
had decided on his educational future.

0	✓
00	*more*
41	
42	
43	
44	
45	
46	
47	
48	
49	
50	
51	
52	
53	
54	
55	

Part 5

For questions **56-65**, read the text below. Use the word given in capitals at the end of each line to form a word that fits in the space in the same line. There is an example at the beginning (**0**).

Changing Mood

One of the most (0) ......*effective*...... ways of changing a person's mood involves	EFFECT
using smells. Aromatherapy, which has been in (56) .... since it was	EXIST
first (57) .... used by the Ancient Egyptians, is now thought to be of	SUCCESS
great (58) .... benefit. Although many people claim that true	PSYCHOLOGY
(59) .... cannot be achieved safely without using aromatherapy, the	RELAX
method is still viewed with (60) .... by the majority who are	SUSPECT
(61) .... from trying it because it is surrounded by a 'mysterious	COURAGE
philosophy'. Today the use of scent to cause a (62) .... in tension or	REDUCE
an increase in the (63) .... to concentrate intensely is made even	ABLE
more effective when it is used in (64) .... with music. The most	COMBINE
important advantage of aromatherapy is its (65) .... Just a few	SIMPLE
drops of oil in a hot bath is said to work wonders.	

Extension and Revision

A Vocabulary Building

Complete the unfinished words in the following sentences which are related to the enviroment and the weather.

1 When the vol.................. erupted l.................. flowed down and buried the town below.
2 Pol.................. is a great problem nowadays, especially the dumping of nuc.................. wa.................. .
3 The heavy rain caused the river to over.................. and the resulting fl.................. destroyed crops.
4 Last night's st.................. was terrible: the thu.................. and lig.................. kept me awake for hours.
5 The lack of rain led to a dro.................. in the region.
6 If we rec.................. paper, fewer for.................. will be cut down.
7 It was so fo.................. that I could hardly make out the road ahead.
8 I was enjoying the cool sea bre.................. when a g.................. of wind blew my hat off.
9 Very strong winds like torn.................. can be highly destructive.
10 Traffic fu.................. , rub.................. dumping and fert .... all pollute the environment.

B Word Use

Use the words on the left to complete the sentences on the right. Make sure the word is in the correct form.

1 **common** / **ordinary** / **regular**

a Once a(n) .... sight, the buffalo is quite rare nowadays.
b You don't need special tools – .... ones will do.
c Soldiers have a(n) .... routine – everything's done at a set time.

2 **broadcast** / **announce** / **spread**

a All she does is .... rumours all day.
b The event will be .... live on national television.
c The names of the winners will be .... next week.

3 **viewers** / **listeners** / **audience** / **spectators**

a .... will be able to hear a live commentary of the big match.
b The .... gave the actors a standing ovation.
c This TV programme offers the .... the chance to win cash prizes.
d The .... were angered by the referee's decisions.

4 **tired** / **bored** / **sick** / **fed up**

a He orders us about all the time. I'm .... with it.
b At first it was interesting, but they soon became .... with it.
c I'm .... and .... of your constant complaints.

5 **owing to** / **according to** / **on account of** / **as regards**

a .... the weather forecast, it will be dry and sunny.
b Harriet was offered the job .... her linguistic abilities.
c .... poor visibility the start of the race was delayed.
d .... pollution, the area is particularly bad.

C Use of Prepositions

Use the prepositions below to complete the sentences which follow.

about   at (x 2)   for (x 2)   in (x 2)   to

1 The new outbreak of cattle disease has put consumers .... risk.
2 We're all quite enthusiastic .... the new project.
3 I'm not very good .... maths, I'm afraid.
4 You must complete this section .... pencil.
5 Our car is not suitable .... off road travel.
6 Everything is included .... the price so you won't have to pay extra.
7 You can't speak to Mr Blake because he left .... Brazil yesterday.
8 I object .... being shouted at for no reason.

D Word Formation

I Use the word in capitals at the end of each sentence to form a word that fits in the space in the sentence.

1 Is there any proof of the .... of UFOs? EXIST
2 He aroused .... by disappearing just after the jewels had been stolen. SUSPECT
3 A .... of hard work and good luck allowed him to reach the top. COMBINE
4 It's the .... of the idea that makes it amazing. SIMPLE
5 She has considerable .... but hardly ever makes us of it. ABLE

II Choose the odd word out from the following groups of words according to how they form nouns.

1	wise	pure	bored	free
2	close	short	carry	marry
3	urgent	transparent	tend	patient
4	honest	deliver	break	jealous
5	realise	analyse	paralyse	emphasise
6	pay	develop	treat	thick

Hints on improving your listening skills I

We often hear but we don't always listen! What is the difference? Unless you are deaf, you will hear everything that is happening around you: noise, music, sounds from nature, speech, etc. If we were to listen to all these things then we would be rather confused. Moreover, when your parents or teachers tell you to do something that you don't really want to do, you hear what is said but you don't listen. Listening means hearing and understanding.

For the exam, therefore, you will need to practise listening rather than just hearing. Often students say after checking their answers in class 'Oh, I **heard** that!' So, if they heard it, why didn't they get the answer right?

Here are a few ideas to help you improve your listening skills:

- Listen to a favourite pop song you have and try to write down the words. If you already have the words, that's even better as you can then check your 'version' with the real song!
- Try to write down things that are being said on TV or on the radio. Start simply – try to write every fifth sentence you hear.
- Again, listening to radio or TV, try to play word games with yourself. Write down all the adjectives you hear for two minutes, or try writing down all the time expressions you hear. When you are good at doing this, try writing down a list of the different tenses you hear over a period of five minutes.

The more you practise listening for a **reason**, the easier it will become for you to understand what you are hearing.

Part 1

You will hear people talking in eight different situations. For questions **1-8**, choose the best answer, **A**, **B** or **C**.

1 You hear two people talking about a TV programme.
What does the woman say about a car featured on the programme?

A It is extremely fast.
B It doesn't start with a key.
C It is very economical.

[ ] **1**

2 You hear part of a radio programme. What is the programme about?

A gardening
B cookery
C motoring

[ ] **2**

3 Listen to a fashion model talking about herself. What does she say?

A You shouldn't let success affect your character.
B She enjoys being in the news all the time.
C You should always make sure your agency is honest.

[ ] **3**

4 Listen to a person talking about how he took up a hobby. What is his hobby?

A collecting souvenirs from Australia
B stamp collecting
C coin collecting

[ ] **4**

5 You hear a man receiving some news. What is his reaction to it?

A He is not very surprised.
B He doesn't believe it.
C He thinks it is a joke.

[ ] **5**

6 You hear a man talking on the phone. Who is he talking to?

A a shop assistant
B a friend
C a TV repair man

[ ] **6**

7 You hear a woman talking to her friend. Why didn't she get the job?

A She arrived late for the interview.
B She didn't have enough experience.
C She wasn't young enough for the position.

[ ] **7**

8 You hear two women discussing a colleague. What is he going to do?

A work for his uncle
B meet the president
C get a better job

[ ] **8**

Part 2

You will hear a football association president talking during a meeting. For questions **9-18**, complete the sentences. You will need to write a word, short phrase or a number in each box.

Organisation

New Clubs

The league has received applications from [ ] **9**

Ten of these teams will join the league [ ] **10**

Season

Teams from Division Three start on Saturday [ ] **11**

Extra games will be arranged before the next [ ] **12**

Next year the total number of league teams will be [ ] **13**

We will be notified of these changes [ ] **14**

The Cup

The Grant Cup starts on Saturday [ ] **15**

In the first round there will be [ ] **16**

First round matches will not include teams from [ ] **17**

Fixture lists can be obtained from [ ] **18**

Part 3

You will hear five different people talking about a teacher they can remember from school. For questions **19-23**, choose which of the teachers **A-F** is being described. Use the letters only once. There is one extra letter which you do not need to use.

A This teacher did not put things across very well.

B This teacher gave the class too much work.

C This teacher physically punished students.

D This teacher actively encouraged students.

E This teacher could not control the students.

F This teacher was not fair to some students.

Speaker 1		**19**
Speaker 2		**20**
Speaker 3		**21**
Speaker 4		**22**
Speaker 5		**23**

Part 4

You will hear part of a radio interview about shopping in the 21st Century. For questions **24-30**, choose the best answer **A**, **B** or **C**.

24 Alison Brown believes that new shopping methods

A will take off immediately.
B will become much more popular when people's opinions change.
C will not replace hypermarkets or supermarkets.

[ ] **24**

25 Many people are frightened that hackers

A will make illegal use of personal information.
B will steal their credit cards.
C will cause damage to their computers.

[ ] **25**

26 It is not easy to sell perfume by the new method because

A the customer can't smell it.
B it's an expensive product.
C it doesn't look nice on a computer screen.

[ ] **26**

27 If you're looking for something unusual,

A you should try your local shops first.
B it's likely to be extremely expensive.
C the new method will save time.

[ ] **27**

28 What does Alison say about the new method of shopping?

A It will force people to go on strike.
B It has caused some people to become unemployed.
C It is too complicated for some people.

[ ] **28**

29 Handicapped people find on-line shopping better because

A it allows them to move around more freely.
B they feel less dependent.
C they can choose what they want to buy.

[ ] **29**

30 Which of the following would an on-line shopper be most likely to purchase?

A a piece of furniture
B a carpet
C a computer game

[ ] **30**

Hints on improving your speaking skills I

In the exam, you will gain marks for good pronunciation and intonation. One way to get better at this is to read aloud to yourself (wait until nobody is home). Check in the mirror to see if you are opening your mouth or swallowing your words.

Get together with a friend who is also taking the exam and record your own voices. Then you can help each other by giving your opinion on which words or phrases were difficult to understand. When you hear your own voice you will also realise that it's not always so easy to understand.

Check how many times you say 'Erm' or 'Ah' while you are speaking in English. If you have to pause for thought before you speak, then take a breath and then speak slowly and clearly rather than saying 'Er ...". You will sound more fluent and the listener (in this case, the examiner) will found your voice more pleasing.

Make up imaginary conversations with yourself and the examiner and practise saying them aloud (again, make sure you are alone when you do this!).

Smile while you are speaking!

Part 1 (About 3 minutes)

Ask and answer the following questions with a partner.

- What kind of sports are you and your friends interested in?
- What kind of music do you enjoy most?
- How do you usually spend your holidays?
- Is there anywhere you would particularly like to visit? Why?
- What is your favourite time of the year? Why?

Part 2 (About 4 minutes)

Practise speaking about the photographs shown on page 182.

Candidate A, here are your two photographs. They show different types of musicians. Please let Candidate B have a look at them. Candidate A, I'd like you to compare and contrast these photographs, saying what you find attractive and unattractive about each of these jobs (approximately one minute).

Candidate B, could you please tell us which of these musicians you would prefer to be (approximately twenty seconds).

Candidate B, here are your two photographs. They show different means of transport. Please let Candidate A have a look at them. Candidate B, I'd like you to compare and contrast these photographs, saying which form of transport is more environmentally-friendly (approximately one minute).

Candidate A, could you please tell us which method of transport you would prefer to use to get to school or work (approximately twenty seconds).

Part 3 (About 3 minutes)

Discuss the following with a partner.

Imagine you take a holiday job looking after people's pets while they are away. Talk to each other about which three unusual pets you would not be prepared to look after from those shown on the opposite page. It is not necessary to agree with each other.

Part 4 (About 4 minutes)

Give each other your opinions about the following questions.

- What are the advantages of having a pet?
- What difficulties can you face when you have a pet?
- How does having a pet make you more responsible?
- Which animals make the best pets?
- What do we use animals for nowadays?

Hints on improving your reading skills II

In our own language we often adopt some reading habits as very young children that are not so useful for us at a later stage. In fact, they might even slow down our reading without us realising it. So, check whether you do any of the following:

Saying the words quietly while reading
We did this as young children and as beginners in the language in order to help our pronunciation and recognition of words. However, if you have continued to do this it will slow down your reading tremendously. Not only that, you run the risk of being accused by your teacher, or the invigilator, of talking or passing on information to other students. Try reading without moving your lips and see how much faster it is.

Using your finger to guide your eyes on the text
Again, in the early lessons you need a guide, especially if the letters of the language are different from your own. Now that you are more experienced, though, you need to give your eyes more freedom. Research has shown that it is quicker to move the eyes down and across the page in 'chunks' rather than reading every word along the line from left to right. If your finger gets in the way, you will slow down. Especially in Part 4 of the Reading paper, you need to move fast through the text. So, start practising!

Going back over what you have read
Of course, you will need to read texts more than once in some cases in order to find and then verify your answer. However, your first reading can be speeded up if you learn to continue reading and not keep going back over previous sentences. Don't read so fast that you cannot understand anything, but read fast enough to get a good grasp of the main points and themes of the text before you answer your questions.

Remember
If you're having trouble building up enthusiasm about reading in English **outside** the classroom, why don't you get your parents to sponsor your reading. You could earn some extra pocket money or give the money to a good cause (or even buy another book!). Your parents, of course, would expect you to give them a brief (oral or written) review of the book or article or magazine you have read!

Happy reading and good luck in the exam!

Part 1

You are going to read a newspaper article about robots. Choose the most suitable heading from the list **A-I** for each part (**1-7**) of the article. There is one extra heading which you do not need to use. There is an example at the beginning (**0**).

A	Meeting a need
B	Showing concern
C	A friendly voice
D	Stay!
E	Caring for its owner
F	Helping with the housework
G	Company and links for the aged
H	Getting it right
I	Perfect company

Robocat

You can pet it, use it as a diary and one day it might even save an elderly person's life.

From our Science Correspondent in Tokyo

0 I

Elderly people who live alone were yesterday promised the ideal companion – a robopet.

1

A Japanese electronics company has responded to the nation's rapidly ageing population by producing a 'talking' animal robot which comes in the shape of a cat, tiger or bear. With sensors in its head and microphones in its ears, the pet can respond to a user's voice and touch. Basic questions, a scratch behind the ears or a pat on the head are rewarded with a response.

2

The pets come programmed with 50 expressions that can be tailored to the individual. Robopet can, for example, announce, 'It's karaoke day – let's sing!' or act as a diary with advice like, 'It's Thursday. Today is your doctor's appointment.' The robot can work out the best time to wake its owner with a cheery 'Good morning' or know when to initiate a conversation if a room is silent.

3

It is expected that senior citizens will make up 27% of Japan's population by 2025. A spokesman for the company, Masushita, said 'The robot not only serves as a comfortable companion but it can also support the elderly users by linking them with welfare organisations or social workers without invading their privacy.'

4

The pet can be connected via a phone line to a network centre where health and social workers are able to send out information while monitoring the aged owner. The robot can even be programmed to alert an elderly person to danger or to ask, 'Are you all right?'

5

And if the pet seems to be initiating conversation but not receiving any response it will react accordingly. It will alert staff at the centre, which is staffed 24 hours a day, so that someone can check up on the owner.

6

It cost Matsushita £12 million over three years to perfect the robot after extensive trials and testing. The company hopes to have it on the market within two years.

7

However, the robots will not be programmed to run around. During market testing, the company discovered that elderly consumers did not want a robot that they would have to chase all over the house!

Part 2

You are going to read an extract from a book about the relationship between humans and other animals. For questions **8-14**, choose the answer **A**, **B**, **C** or **D** which you think fits best according to the text.

Man has viewed other species of animals in many different lights. He has looked on them as predators, prey, partners, pests and pets. He has exploited them economically, studied them scientifically, appreciated them aesthetically and exaggerated them symbolically. Above all, he has competed with them for living space, dominated them, and all too often exterminated them.

From his earliest days he has feared certain species as killers. Some, such as lions, tigers, wolves, crocodiles, giant snakes and sharks have been pictured as savage man-eaters, hungry for human flesh. Others have been labelled as aggressive poisoners – the venomous snakes, deadly spiders, scorpions and stinging insects. In every case he has magnified the true dangers. None of the supposed man-eaters has ever had mankind as a main course on its menu. Only on very rare occasions and under special circumstances have they turned to human flesh, as a tasty addition to their natural diet. Big cats that have taken up man-eating have nearly always done so because of injury or illness. A wounded leopard, unable to catch its usual, fast-moving prey, may be driven to seeking food in a native village in the form of a human victim. When this happens, word spreads quickly and in no time at all leopards everywhere are under attack as potential man-killers. Wolves have been even more unjustly condemned as a bloodthirsty enemy of man. Endless, bloodcurdling stories have been told about them, but hardly ever have they been authenticated. In an area in America where such stories were common, a reward was once offered for any case of an unprovoked attack on man. The reward has never been claimed. Everywhere myth has dominated fact, and the wolf is almost extinct.

In a similar way, poisonous animals have been described as a major threat, attacking man whenever possible. Again, fiction has overwhelmed fact. No poisonous snake attacks: it merely defends itself. It needs its venom to kill or paralyse its prey which it then swallows whole... Since no venomous snake is large enough to swallow even a small human baby whole, it follows that to strike at a human target is a waste of precious venom. It is a course of action that is only taken as a last resort, in a desperate attempt at self-protection. This has not stopped snakes becoming the most feared and hated of all animals. They are destroyed ruthlessly wherever they are encountered.

Prey species have also suffered but in a rather different way. Instead of being hunted to extinction, they have been transformed into domestic breeds. With the great switch from hunting to farming which took place about ten thousand years ago, the most important prey species were brought under human control and herded, penned and killed at will. Selective breeding gradually changed them. As food animals they became more docile and they carried more meat. The result was a dramatic reduction in the number of animal species on the human menu. Whereas the early hunters killed anything they could catch, and ate a wide variety of animals, the farmers and their descendants, right down to the present day, have restricted their 'prey' to relatively few types: mostly goats, sheep, pigs, cattle, rabbits, chickens, geese and ducks.

8 How have people regarded animals?

A in one way in particular
B as things to be exploited
C in several different ways
D as creatures we share the planet with

9 What does 'others' in line 14 refer to?

A people
B poisoners
C animals
D man-eaters

10 In what circumstances would an animal be most likely to kill and eat a human?

A if it wasn't able to catch the animals it normally ate
B if it was attacked by a person
C if someone tried to capture it
D if someone built a home in its territory

11 What is meant by 'bloodcurdling' in line 33?

A amusing
B particularly frightening
C ridiculous
D very interesting

12 Why is the snake's venom described as 'precious' in line 45?

A The snake needs it to survive.
B It is worth a lot of money.
C It can be used to save lives by making medicine.
D It is extremely rare.

13 How did the animals kept on farms change?

A They became heavier.
B They developed fewer teeth.
C They became more attractive.
D They started to eat anything they were given.

14 What does the writer think of man's behaviour towards animals?

A It is natural.
B It is justified.
C It is unfair.
D It is improving.

Part 3

You are going to read a newspaper article about airline seats. Eight sentences have been removed from the article. Choose from the sentences **A-I** the one which fits each gap (**15-21**). There is one extra sentence which you do not need to use. There is an example at the beginning (**0**).

Airline Seat 'Danger'

New space restrictions in economy class may be life-threatening

Cramped seating in the economy-class sections of aeroplanes is not just uncomfortable but potentially life-threatening, according to a report in the medical journal the *Lancet*. **0** I

A study of 24 doctors on a long-haul flight found that only two out of eighteen in economy class could adopt the brace position recommended on the plane's safety card – and they were the smallest of the group. **15** ____ The authors of the report – from the Neunkirchen Hospital and the Department of Emergency Medicine at the University of Vienna – are now calling for greater space between seat rows to increase safety.

16 ____ 'We don't think it is a safety issue,' he said. 'We have rigorous cabin evacuation and safety standards and all UK aircraft meet them.'

In a blaze of publicity in the past week, both British Airways and Virgin Atlantic introduced sleeper seats, boasting unparallelled comfort in the front cabins of their planes. **17** ____

Until recently, economy class was at least 'bearable' – with an 86 centimetre seat pitch and padded chairs. Scheduled airlines such as BA, KLM and Lufthansa gave passengers decent leg room and comfortable seats. **18** ____ Extra rows

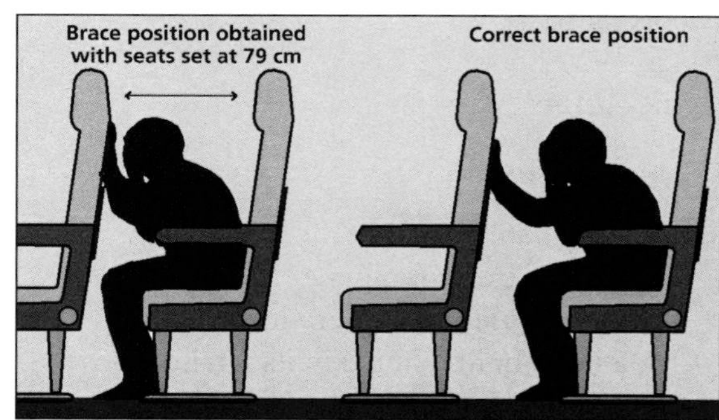

have been put into the cabin, with the result that the average seat pitch now is 79 centimetres.

19 ____ It announced free champagne for economy passengers last September, but at the same time reduced leg room by 8 centimetres to a 79 centimetre pitch.

Virgin Atlantic packs more seats on to its Florida-bound aircraft than it does on other routes. British Airways flies some of its 777s with more seats across the cabin than others. **20** ____ New Zealand boasts the roomiest economy seats and the greatest comfort with 46-centimetre wide seats and more leg room.

21 ____ Some charter airlines even offer the opportunity to upgrade – at a price – to seats which, at 86-91 centimetres, are roomier than those of most scheduled airlines.

A Economy class on scheduled airlines is now often little better than economy on charter flights.

B But space gained by the few is space lost in economy.

C Some passengers have complained about being bent double on long haul flights.

D All six of their fellow passengers travelling in first class could adopt the position, which is internationally recognised as improving the chances of survival in the event of a crash.

E Singapore Airlines has become the latest carrier to scale down its seats.

F But the arrival of new, weight-saving seats caused economy class to take a turn for the worse.

G A spokesman for the Civil Aviation Authority, which is responsible for safety on all British planes, denied that cramped conditions were a threat to passengers.

H The seats are just 43 centimetres wide.

I Space has become so tight that passengers cannot brace themselves to protect head and limbs in the event of a crash.

Part 4

You are going to read six extracts about flu and its treatment. For questions **22-35**, choose from the extracts **A-F**. The extracts may be chosen more than once. There is an example at the beginning (**0**). Mark your answers on the separate answer sheet.

Which person

says spending a lot on flu products is illogical?	**0** D	
has recently got over a flu attack?	**22**	
states that people have been spending more on flu products?	**23**	
describes why people start coughing?	**24**	
says buying expensive flu products is a waste of money?	**25**	
says most flu products contain ingredients for many symptoms?	**26**	
implies that just taking medicine improves the way someone feels?	**27**	**28**
says the most effective treatment requires no medicine?	**29**	
says you shouldn't make others ill?	**30**	
says cold and flu products do not cure people?	**31**	**32**
says flu products can cause problems for the patient?	**33**	
suggests you should take something for a sore throat?	**34**	
says people aren't forced to buy cold and flu products?	**35**	

Flu Drugs Exposed as a Waste of Money

A Andrew Hexheimer, pharmacologist

The trouble with many flu products is that they have something for several symptoms. As a result, people who don't have those symptoms – for example, one that is for aches and pains when they only have a sore throat – and they are therefore much more likely to get side effects.

B Simon Frad, doctor

A cough is simply dryness in the throat and a build-up of debris in the lung. The only way to cure it is by getting humidity into the lungs. Instead of taking medicine, the best cure is to boil a kettle and put your head over a bowl of steaming water. We are spending too much on the wrong products. The best thing you can do is grab a couple of bottles of cheap painkillers and a throat lozenge or two, and take to your bed until the illness has passed.

C Joe Collier, professor

You should stay indoors, keep warm and stop spreading the virus. That is what I did last week when I had flu and it worked just fine. As for remedies, I wouldn't waste money on all these fancy treatments. A 32-capsule packet of aspirin costs about 50p, and that is all you need. Take those. Forget about anything else. You are just throwing away hard-earned cash.

D Alan Hay, doctor

We are not getting the right medicines. A bottle of inexpensive painkillers should do the trick. However, I think that if you choose one of the more expensive treatments, which typically cost between £2 and £4 for a packet of between 12 and 20 capsules, you are not using logic. But if someone thinks they feel better after taking these treatments, then I would say: Why not?

E Claire Gillen, company pharmacist

There has been a significant increase in the sale of cold and flu products, but our remedies are intended merely to treat symptoms. They don't cure colds. There are certainly cases when a cheap bottle of aspirin would be just as effective. Indeed, we even recommend steam inhalation as well as bed rest and fluids.

F Mark White, pharmaceutical manufacturer

No one says that over-the-counter medicines are going to cure colds or flu. They are merely designed to help people feel better. All our claims about our products are backed by scientific research. In any case we sell aspirin as well, so we give customers a choice.

Hints on writing a report

A report is usually written for a specific target reader and is a formal document that you might prepare for a headmaster, an organisation, or a business person, for example.

Approach
Read the question very carefully and list the points that you have been asked to write about. You will need to expand your notes, as you are expected to provide detailed information in a report. Order your notes:

Introduction	State why you are writing and what the report contains.
Main body	Presentation of the information. You can write short points (which are numbered, lettered or bulleted), or you can give your information in two or three paragraphs that have headings for the reader to see clearly where to look for specific information.
Conclusion	May include your opinion, recommendation or suggestions.

Pre-exam preparation
Plenty of practice writing reports! It is not advisable to select this option in the exam if you have not already had experience writing reports. Your teacher will be able to show you in advance several different styles of report.

Remember
The language of a report is usually formal, so do not use contractions and try to avoid using personal pronouns. Don't forget to use some more formal connectors like 'Moreover', 'In addition to ...', 'Furthermore,' etc.

Hints on answering questions for the set books

Don't attempt this question if you have not studied the book. Reading the book just for pleasure will be good for your English, but you will not be able to answer the questions well with only one reading.

It's a good idea to make notes on the following aspects of any book you read:

Theme
You can note the main theme of the book and any sub-themes that you come across by chapter. Make notes about how the theme is developed in the book.

Character(s)
Make a list of all the characters and a few notes about their personalities, special features, etc. Make a note of the relationships between characters as well as their attitudes towards each other.

Plot
Make brief notes about how the plot develops and where the key points are.

Setting
Make a note of where particular actions take place and how the place relates to the plot, or if the setting has any direct influence on any of the characters.

In addition to this, you should have some thoughts about the title of the book and the cover design.

Pre-exam preparation
If there is a film or video that goes with the book, then it would be a good idea to arrange to see it. You can compare the film version with the book and see what details were left out or added. The visual aid will help you remember scenes in the book.

Remember
Reading should be enjoyable. You can read all the set books if you like, and you're not obliged to answer the question in the exam!! Whatever reading you do will help you with your overall ability to understand and express yourself well in English.

Part 1

You **must** answer this question.

1 You went on an eight-day holiday to three capital cities in Europe. Unfortunately you were not satisfied with the holiday and did not enjoy it. Read the holiday advertisement and the notes you made below about the holiday. Then, using this information, write a letter to the organisers, complaining about the holiday and asking what the organisers intend to do about your complaint.

Three capital cities on one great tour

Super hotels | City tours | Luxury coach travel | Fully escorted

8 days from £399

Fly from London, Liverpool, Manchester or Glasgow

Here's the chance to visit three fascinating European capitals on one superb holiday by luxury coach. You'll fly to Munich, where you spend the first night. Then, over the next seven days, you'll see spectacular scenery and discover historic delights. You'll stay in three-star standard hotels, enjoy free city tours and have the services of an experienced guide.

Hotels – had to share room with two others
– poor service
Tours – they wanted extra for the free tours!
– very short – didn't see much
– guides couldn't speak English!!
Coach – air conditioning broke down – hot!!
ACTION What do they intend to do? Money back? or ...

Write a **letter** of between **120** and **180** words in an appropriate style. Do not write any addresses.

Part 2

Write an answer to **one** of the questions **2-5** in this part. Write your answer in **120-180** words in an appropriate style.

2 An international young people's magazine is investigating the question:

Are all the subjects taught at school really necessary?

Write your **article** for the magazine.

3 You have decided to enter a short story competition. The competition rules say that the story must begin with the following words:

I waited for a moment before ringing the doorbell.

Write your **story** for the competition.

4 You have just seen this advertisement on your school noticeboard.

AU PAIR EXCHANGE

Wanted:
Young students 16-18 years old to work with friendly families in the south of England during the months of July and August. Improve your English and earn some pocket money at the same time.

If you are interested, apply in writing, describing your character and telling us about any previous experience. Let us know why you think you would benefit from an au pair exchange. In your letter, mention knowledge of any other languages. Your letter must be accompanied by a letter of approval from your parent or guardian.

Write your **letter** of application. Do not write any addresses.

5 Background reading texts

Answer **one** of the following two questions based on your reading of **one** of the set books. Your answer should contain enough detail to make it clear to someone who may not have read the book.

Either (a) Imagine that you are one of the main characters in the book and you are going to be interviewed. Write a **composition**, stating what questions you would expect to be asked and how you would answer them.

or (b) In your opinion, which character must be the most satisfied with the way the book ends. Write a **composition**, giving reasons for your choice.

Hints on improving your Use of English skills

From the beginning of your course, you should have been building up a lot of notes with vocabulary, useful expressions and collocations, phrasal verbs, etc. Before the exam it is a good idea to re-order your notes, and plan your revision hours.

During the year you should aim to do some revision with a friend. Practise writing short Use of English tasks for each other and then see where you have problems. You can ask your teacher to give you some helpful explanations, if one particular problem keeps occurring.

Read, read, read! Whatever you can put your hands on – read it! Everything you read will help you to predict the types of language that you are going to be presented with in the exam. Remember that most of the texts in the Use of English paper are taken from magazine articles or newspapers and have been modified for the exam. The examiners also try to keep up-to-date with changing topics and trends, so reading in your own language will help you to prepare for the types of material you will come across.

Part 1

For questions **1-15**, read the text below and decide which answer **A**, **B**, **C** or **D** best fits each space. There is an example at the beginning (**0**).

Example:

0 **A** for **B** about **C** on **D** from

0	A	B	C	D
	▭	▬	▭	▭

Living Longer

When Shakespeare wrote (0) .... the *Seven Ages of Man*, living beyond sixty years of age was rare. Those who did were (1) .... to be wise and deserving of respect.

Now, the (2) .... age of the population of Britain is (3) .... relatively quickly. In 1961, 6.2 million people in Britain were aged 65 or over. Today, the figure is just (4) .... 9 million, but the biggest increase has been seen in the over-eighty age (5) ...., which has doubled since 1961.

In many respects this is a welcome trend. There are numerous instances of old people doing remarkable things. For example, Elsa Scotchmer, 104, (6) .... up travelling at 96 years of age and Hildegarde Ferrera made a parachute jump at the age of 99. This means that the youth of today may be able to look (7) .... to a hundred years of active life, especially with the medical (8) .... of the 21st Century producing human spare parts grown from cell tissue in (9) .... instead of drugs.

On the other hand, there is a fear that the economy will be unable to (10) .... the aged. Although this is logical, it is not (11) .... the most serious problem. It is believed that the real problem will be one of attitude (12) .... the aged. At least thirty years of active life after (13) .... will be a (14) .... new concept and the function of the aged in (15) .... will have to be revised. In short, the aged will not be as old as they feel, but as old as other people feel they are.

1	**A**	regarded	**B**	looked	**C**	indicated	**D**	considered
2	**A**	average	**B**	medium	**C**	normal	**D**	common
3	**A**	raising	**B**	growing up	**C**	rising	**D**	lifting
4	**A**	lower	**B**	less	**C**	fewer	**D**	under
5	**A**	set	**B**	group	**C**	team	**D**	range
6	**A**	started	**B**	took	**C**	got	**D**	went
7	**A**	up	**B**	ahead	**C**	forward	**D**	onward
8	**A**	rebellion	**B**	revolt	**C**	improvement	**D**	revolution
9	**A**	factories	**B**	companies	**C**	studios	**D**	laboratories
10	**A**	hold	**B**	support	**C**	maintain	**D**	bear
11	**A**	necessarily	**B**	possibly	**C**	likely	**D**	obviously
12	**A**	towards	**B**	opposite	**C**	against	**D**	with
13	**A**	redundancy	**B**	pension	**C**	retirement	**D**	dismissal
14	**A**	certainly	**B**	completely	**C**	basically	**D**	fully
15	**A**	society	**B**	public	**C**	civilisation	**D**	community

Part 2

For questions **16-30**, read the text below and think of the word which best fits each space. Use only one word in each space. There is an example at the beginning (**0**).

A New Kind of Hotel

Owing (0) ......to....... a sudden drop in tourism after ten years of incredible growth, hotel owners have (16) .... forced to find new ways of attracting tourists.

The latest trend is to make bigger, (17) .... luxurious hotels. As a (18) .... , many new hotels of this type, the biggest and most expensive of (19) .... is the £1 billion *Bellagio Hotel* in Las Vegas, have appeared (20) .... over the world. The *Bellagio* is 36 storeys high with 3,025 rooms and 400 luxury suites. In (21) .... to the luxurious rooms, the hotel (22) .... decorated with a £200 million art collection, including works by famous artists (23) .... as Van Gogh, Renoir and Picasso. There is also an eleven-acre lake in (24) .... of the hotel.

Prices at the hotel are probably (25) .... expensive for most people so the hotel is aiming to attract rich clients. Rooms cost up to £300 (26) .... night and the slot machines in the casino are £650 a go.

Casino owner, Steve Wynne, (27) .... idea the hotel was, realises that it is a gamble but he is prepared to (28) .... the risk and he is not alone. The *Venetian* hotel, which is in the (29) .... city as the *Bellagio*, has rooms that are at (30) .... 75 m^2 and has copies of St Marks Square and the Grand Canal.

Part 3

For questions **31-40**, complete the second sentence so that it has a similar meaning to the first sentence, using the word given. **Do not change the word given**. You must use between two and five words including the word given. There is an example at the beginning (**0**).

0 It is the strangest music I have ever heard.
never

I have .... music.

The gap can be filled by the words 'never heard such strange' so you write:

0	*never heard such strange*

31 Jim doesn't take criticism very easily.
hard

It .... take criticism.

32 Roberta has invited me to her party.
given

I .... to Roberta's party.

33 They visit us occasionally.
time

We see .... time.

34 Carla had the ability to beat her opponent, but she was still recovering from the flu.
could

Carla .... the game, if she hadn't been recovering from the flu.

35 Despite Roger's bitter complaints about safety, nothing was done.
complained

Even .... about safety, nothing was done.

36 David said he was willing to live alone.
mind

David said he .... his own.

37 I only refused because he was so rude.
if

I wouldn't have refused .... so rude.

38 I'll teach her, but she must make a promise to study hard.
long

I'll teach her .... to study hard.

39 Ken and I were at university together.
same

Ken went .... I did.

40 My parents always want me to turn off my television at midnight.
let

My parents .... television after midnight.

Part 4

For questions **41-55**, read the text below and look carefully at each line. Some of the lines are correct and some have a word which should not be there. If a line is correct put a tick (✓) by the number. If a line has a word which should not be there, write the word. There are two examples at the beginning (**0** and **00**).

Solving Personal Problems

0 It may sound strange but the only personal problems that I
00 am unable to solve are of my own. Since I am a good listener,
41 I am often asked for my opinion when I discuss about other
42 people's problems with them. Most of the time the advice
43 I give is valuable so that they have no hesitation in coming
44 and explaining me what is bothering them. I think I am
45 good at telling others what exactly they have to do because
46 I can look at their problems objectively. On the other one
47 hand, my own problems seem to be far more than difficult
48 to solve. For example, when I am forced to make a choice I just
49 think about what I'd rather to do without giving any
50 thought to the consequences. This has often been resulted
51 in me making terrible decisions which have caused to me a
52 lot of trouble. Now that I realise where I am going wrong,
53 I am too determined to do something about it. A friend
54 suggested me that I should write down my problem and
55 try to look at it as if it was somebody else's. I haven't tried
it yet but it seems to be quite a logical suggestion.

0	✓
00	of
41	
42	
43	
44	
45	
46	
47	
48	
49	
50	
51	
52	
53	
54	
55	

Part 5

For questions **56-65**, read the text below. Use the word given in capitals at the end of each line to form a word that fits in the space in the same line. There is an example at the beginning (**0**). Write your word on the separate answer sheet.

Two Points of View

To the (0) ......*amazement*...... of a large majority of concerned parents, yet	AMAZE
another report has failed to come up with (56) .... proof that	CONCLUDE
children are affected by television (57) .... or, more generally,	VIOLENT
what they see on TV or in films. (58) .... who compiled the	RESEARCH
latest report have reached the (59) .... conclusion that children	SURPRISE
can tell the difference between fiction and (60) ...., which	REAL
prevents them from being negatively (61) .... by what they see.	INFLUENCE
The report has received a great deal of (62) .... from people who	CRITICISE
claim that (63) .... films like *Babe* prove the exact opposite.	SENTIMENT
When *Babe*, the story of a talking piglet, came out, (64) .... of	SELL
pork fell (65) ...., proving there is a close connection between	DRAMA
what people see and their reactions to it.	

Extension and Revision

A Vocabulary Building

Complete the unfinished words in the following sentences which are all related to the theme of work.

1 There was so much work at the fa.................. that we were asked to work over.................. .
2 I went for an inter.................. but was told that I didn't have enough exp.................. .
3 Alvin was sa.................. for being late all the time and now he's un.................. .
4 The sal.................. is excellent, your coll.................. are supportive and the bene.................. are marvellous. What more could you want?
5 They'll call a st.................. if the management and the un.................. leaders can't reach an agreement.
6 If the deal goes through hundreds of workers will be made red.................. .
7 I can't ret.................. until I'm sixty because I won't get a good pen.......... if I do.
8 As a repres.................., you will receive a generous travel all.................. .
9 A car.................. in advert.................. sounds exciting.
10 Brian res.................. from the company because he wasn't getting enough comm.................. on the sales he made.

B Word Use

Use the words on the left to complete the sentences on the right. Make sure the word is in the correct form.

1 **regard** / **look** / **consider**
a Kasparov is .... to be the world's best chess player.
b We've always .... on Brian as one of the family.
c I don't .... his excuse as legitimate.

2 **raise** / **grow up** / **rise**
a The balloon .... high into the air before it disappeared.
b She was .... by her aunt.
c Mary .... in Lancashire and then moved to Bath.

3 **set** / **group** / **team**
a There was a small .... of people waiting for the ferry.
b Each department has its own .... of rules.
c The .... of doctors performing the operation was headed by Professor Clarke.

4 **redundancy** / **pension** / **retirement** / **dismissal**
a Part of the company is going to close and many workers face ....
b He's two years away from .... and he's looking forward to it.
c It was her attitude towards the clients that led to her ....
d They get by on a small ....

5 **society** / **public** / **civilisation**
a I wouldn't do that in .... if I were you.
b Two weeks on a desert island is perfect for someone who wishes to escape from ....
c The problems within .... cannot be solved by politicians alone.

C Use of Prepositions

Use the prepositions below to complete the sentences which follow.

for *from* *in* *of (x 2)* *on* *towards* *with*

1 She has a rather peculiar attitude .... strangers.
2 I'm afraid we have nothing .... common.
3 She has great skill combined .... an ability to make people listen.
4 They suspect her .... blackmail.
5 They were criticised .... acting without permission.
6 He's not in the habit .... lying.
7 We still phone each other .... time to time.
8 I suppose I'll just have to do the work .... my own.

D Word Formation

I Use the word in capitals at the end of each sentence to form a word that fits in the space in the sentence.

1 It was a .... end to an unusual day. SURPRISE
2 You should face .... – you'll never be a millionaire. REAL
3 The watch may not be valuable but it's of great .... value. SENTIMENT
4 These shorts were on .... at half price so I bought two pairs. SELL
5 The match ended .... with three goals in the last five minutes. DRAMA

II Choose the odd word out from the following groups of words according to how they form verbs (A) and adverbs (B).

A1	straight	short	list	dark
A2	courage	able	wide	danger
A3	sure	terror	identity	clear
A4	modern	long	apology	emphasis
B1	hard	bad	straight	late
B2	automatic	rude	wise	careless

Hints on improving your listening skills II

It takes a lot of patience to be a good listener. All too often when we are listening (during conversations with others), we are mentally preparing our own response. What happens then is that we don't listen properly. This also happens in the exam. First we have to read the questions properly and then we really have to listen. We need to concentrate. Don't let outside sounds distract you. If somebody laughs because the text is funny, don't join in – stay serious and keep your concentration.

During the year, practise listening by asking a friend if you can summarise what they have been saying. Ask them to give you feedback on the accuracy of your summary.

Practise listening to two or three sentences and then trying to write down the first sentence while continuing to listen to the rest of a text. This will help your concentration and your ability to write and listen at the same time.

Part 1

You will hear people talking in eight different situations. For questions **1-8**, choose the best answer, **A**, **B** or **C**.

1 You hear a man talking about a recent trip. What kind of trip was it?

A a fishing trip
B a shopping trip
C a business trip

1

2 You hear a woman talking about an exam she took. How did she feel immediately afterwards?

A ashamed
B proud
C embarrassed

2

3 You hear two people talking about a party. Who is having the party?

A the man's friend
B the man's boss
C the man's accountant

3

4 You hear a woman talking about a favour she's been asked to do for a person called Sheena. Who is Sheena?

A her cousin
B her niece
C her sister-in-law

4

5 You hear three people talking about travel arrangements. Why can't they go by coach?

A It's too expensive.
B The journey would be tiring.
C There isn't a coach at the right time.

5

6 You hear a woman talking while you are visiting a college. What does she teach?

A history
B art
C physics

6

7 You hear a man talking in the street. Who is he talking to?

A a doctor
B an optician
C a neighbour

7

8 You hear a man talking about a job he's doing. When will the job be finished?

A in one week's time
B a week later than originally planned
C on 12th June

8

Part 2

You will hear a telephone conversation between a catering company and a customer. For questions **9-18**, complete the order form. You will need to write a word, short phrase or a number in each box.

Dimitra's of Knowsley

Name:		**9**
Address:		**10**
	Knowsley	
Telephone:		**11**
Number of guests:		**12**
Menu:	G~~o~~ld*/Premier/Ro~~y~~ale*	
Date:		**13**
Discount: Yes / No* at	%	**14**
Total cost per person:		**15**
Reception to be held:		**16**
Extras:		**17**
Notes:		
*Phone between	*and*	**18**

Part 3

You will hear five different people talking about a past experience. For questions **19-23**, choose which of the activities **A–F** is being described. Use the letters only once. There is one extra letter which you do not need to use.

A taking part in a TV show

B singing in public

C acting in a play

D giving evidence at a trial

E playing in an international tournament

F giving a talk

Speaker 1		19
Speaker 2		20
Speaker 3		21
Speaker 4		22
Speaker 5		23

Part 4

You will hear a conversation about public transport. Answer questions **24-30** by writing
E (for Eric)
W (for Wendy) or
C (for Carol) in the boxes provided.

24	Who didn't know about the strike?	24
25	Who didn't get into work at the usual time?	25
26	Who did something that is prohibited?	26
27	Who decided not to remain silent in a difficult situation?	27
28	Who is greatly surprised?	28
29	Who believes there is a simple solution to problems faced on public transport?	29
30	Who says that we should not only think about the present?	30

Hints on improving your speaking skills II

There are many books on techniques for improving your voice, but a few basic tips will help your performance in the exam room.

Are you breathing?
If you are too nervous, the chances are that you are not breathing correctly. Sit comfortably on your chair and breathe from the stomach and not just from the top of your chest. Your shoulders should not move up and down! Good posture will help you to speak more clearly and confidently.

Are you opening your mouth?
Using the tongue, lips and jaw properly will contribute to better articulation and pronunciation. Check any sounds that cause you difficulty because they don't appear in your own language. Practise these.

Are you using your hands?
Gestures of the face or hands are also part of communication and will help you to improve your intonation. Try reading a passage from a book with a serious face and without moving your hands (record your voice while doing this). Then read the same passage again, but this time imagine you are reading to an audience and let your face and hands also convey your message (recording your voice at the same time). Play back the recordings. Can you hear the difference?

Be natural, be happy and good luck!

Part 1 (About 3 minutes)

Ask and answer the following questions with a partner.

- What do you hope to do in the next few years?
- How important is English in your future plans?
- What do you hope to be doing in five years' time?
- Where would you like to live in the future? Why?
- What is your main ambition?

Part 2 (About 4 minutes)

Practise speaking about the photographs shown on page 183.

Candidate A, here are your two photographs. They show different places to live. Please let Candidate B have a look at them. Candidate A, I'd like you to compare and contrast these photographs, saying what you think the advantages and disadvantages of living in these houses might be (approximately one minute).

Candidate B, could you please tell us which of these houses you would like to live in (approximately twenty seconds).

Candidate B, here are your two photographs. They show two couples sharing a happy moment. Please let Candidate A have a look at them. Candidate B, I'd like you to compare and contrast these photographs, saying what are the biggest differences in relations when people are younger and when they are older (approximately one minute).

Candidate A, could you please tell us which of these situations you would find the most romantic (approximately twenty seconds).

Part 3 (About 3 minutes)

Discuss the following with a partner.

Imagine that the local council has decided to make a new children's playground. On the opposite page is a plan of the part of town where the play ground is going to be built. Talk to each other about which would be the best place A, B or C for the playground to be built. It is not necessary to agree with each other.

Part 4 (About 4 minutes)

Give each other your opinions about the following questions.

- How important is it for children to play with others of their own age?
- How do people usually choose their friends?
- What qualities do you expect in a friend?
- Why do people change their friends?
- Who has the most influence on a person, friends or family?

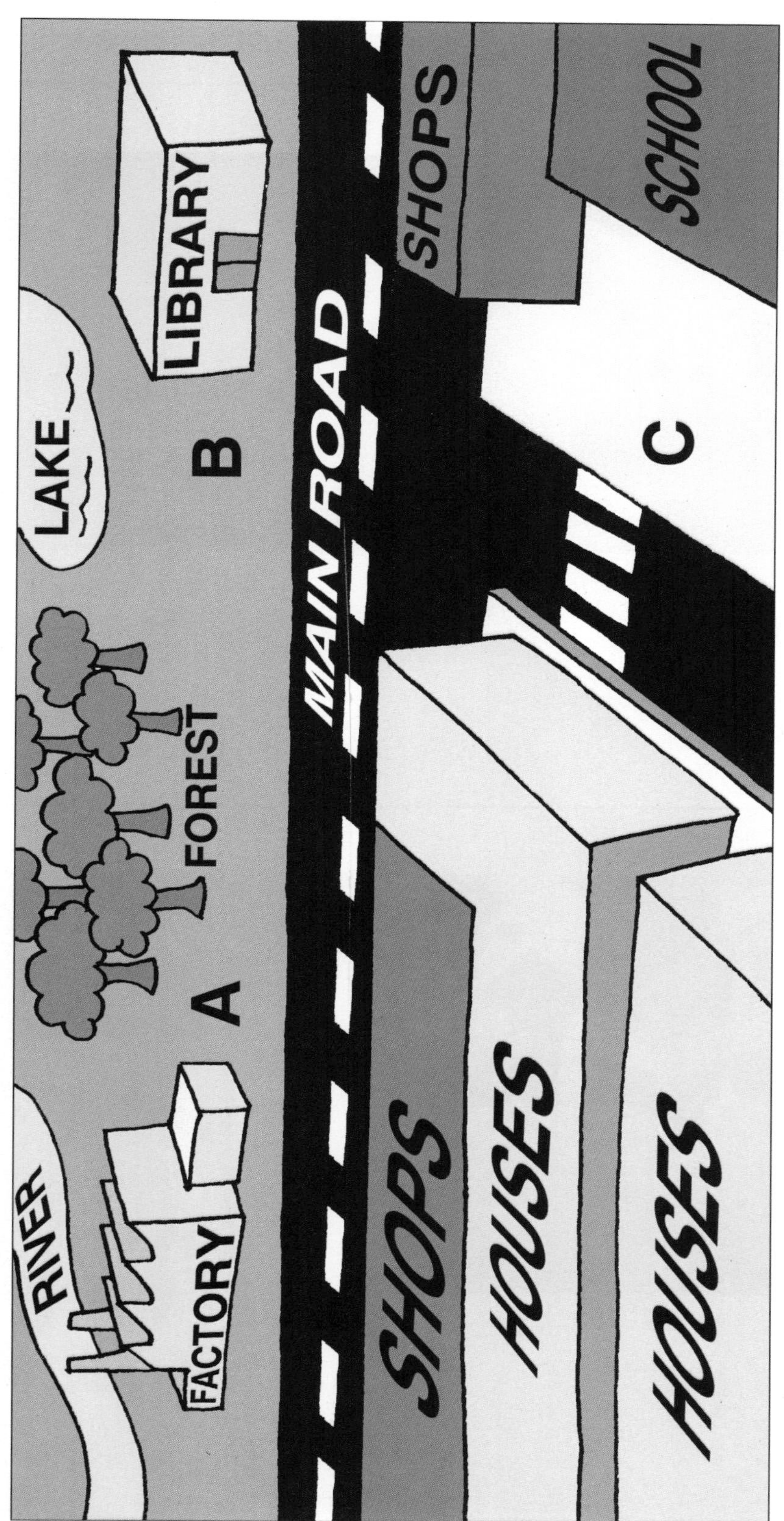

RIVER
FACTORY
A
FOREST
LAKE
B
LIBRARY
MAIN ROAD
SHOPS
SHOPS
HOUSES
HOUSES
C
SCHOOL

Candidate A

Candidate B

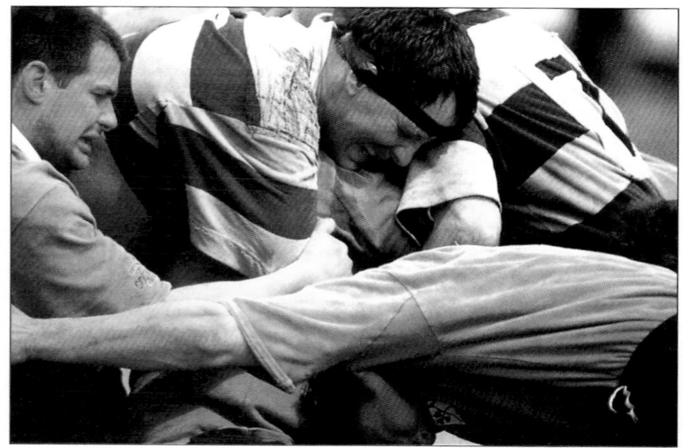

Candidate A

Candidate B

Candidate A

Candidate B

Candidate A

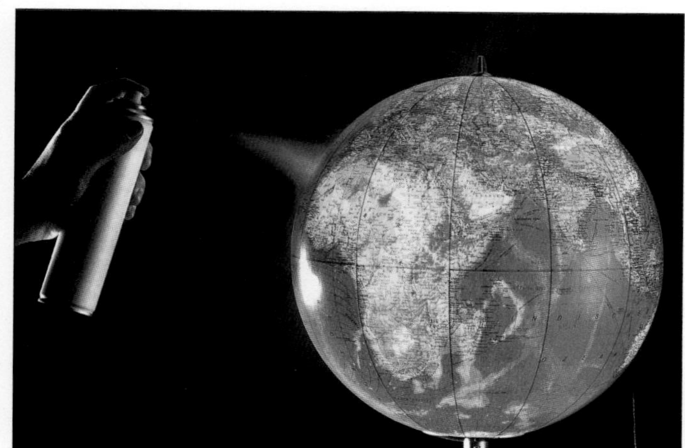

Candidate B

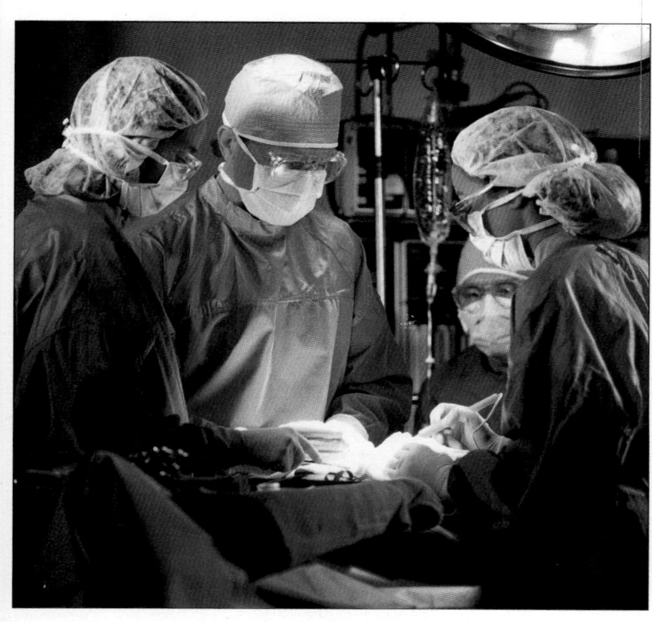

Candidate A

Candidate B

Candidate A

Candidate B

First published by New Editions 1999 – 0504

New Editions
37 Bagley Wood Road
Kennington
Oxford OX1 5LY
England

New Editions
PO Box 76101
171 10 Nea Smyrni
Athens
Greece

Tel.: (+30) 210 9883156
Fax: (+30) 210 9880223
E-mail: enquiries@new-editions.com
Website: www.new-editions.com

ISBN 960-7609-58-1 Student's Book
ISBN 960-7609-59-X Teacher's Book

Acknowledgements

The publishers would like to thank Visual Hellas for permission to reproduce copyright photographs.

The publishers and author would like to thank Sue Emery for patiently preparing the manuscript, and for her careful editing work and contribution to the examination notes and hints.

Illustrations by Sonia Mendi and George Alexandris.

Every effort has been made to trace copyright holders. If any have been inadvertently overlooked, the publishers will be pleased to make the necessary acknowledgements at the first opportunity.